Carolyn McCoy
443 Turner Road
McDonough, GA 30252-2876

MW00785487

Heritage Hymnal
Heart-Warming Favorites

LARGE PRINT EDITION

Compiled and Edited by
James Hawkins and Sharron Lyon

GENEVOX

ISBN 0-7673-3179-6

Foreword

The HERITAGE HYMNAL is a collection of familiar hymns and gospel songs which have stood the test of time. These heart-warming favorites are included in this collection as the result of survey information gathered from Adult Chautauquas and from representative churches across our country. It is our hope that you will enjoy singing from the HERITAGE HYMNAL in personal worship and in worship with other believers.

This hymnal is dedicated to my father, Richard Lyon, whose home-going occurred during production of this collection. It was he who taught me most of these wonderful songs as I accompanied him on the piano. Precious memories!

Sharron Lyon, *Editor*

Production Staff:
Jere Adams, Mickey Goodman, James Hawkins, Linda Konig, Sharron Lyon,
Ed Maksimowicz, Crystal Waters Mangrum, DeAnna Penton, Connie Powell

Beulah Land

EDGAR PAGE STITES

JOHN R. SWENEY

1. I've reached the land of joy di - vine, And all its beau - ty now is mine;
2. The Sav - ior comes and walks with me, And sweet com - mu - nion here have we;
3. A sweet per - fume up - on the breeze Is borne from ev - er ver - nal trees,
4. The zeph - yrs seem to float to me, Sweet sounds of heav - en's mel - o - dy,

Here shines un - dimmed one bliss - ful day, For all my night has passed a - way.
He gen - tly leads me with His hand, For this is heav - en's bor - der - land.
And flow'rs that nev - er fad - ing grow Where streams of life for - ev - er flow.
As an - gels, with the white - robed throng, Join in the sweet re - demp - tion song.

O Beu - lah Land, sweet Beu - lah Land, As on thy high - est mount I stand,

I look a - way a - cross the sea, Where man - sions are pre - pared for me,

And view the shin - ing glo - ry shore, My heav'n, my home for - ev - er - more.

Never Alone

2

Anonymous

Anonymous
Arranged by B. B. McKinney

1. I've seen the light-ning flash - ing, And heard the thun-der roll,
2. The world's fierce winds are blow - ing, Temp - ta-tions are sharp and keen;
3. When in af - flic - tion's val - ley, I'm tread-ing the road of care,
4. He died for me on the moun - tain, For me they pierced His side,

Refrain: No, nev-er a - lone! No, nev-er a - lone!

I've felt sin's break - ers dash - ing, Try-ing to con-quer my soul;
I feel a peace in know - ing My Sav - ior stands be - tween;
My Sav - ior helps me to car - ry My cross when heav-y to bear;
For me He o-pened that foun - tain, The crim - son, cleans - ing tide;

He prom - ised nev - er to leave me, Nev - er to leave me a - lone.

I've heard the voice of Je - sus, Tell - ing me still to fight on,
He stands to shield me from dan - ger, When earth-ly friends are gone,
My feet, en - tan-gled with bri - ars, Read - y to cast me down;
For me He wait-eth in glo - ry, Seat - ed up - on His throne;

No, nev-er a - lone! No, nev-er a - lone!

D.C. for Refrain

He prom - ised nev - er to leave me, Nev - er to leave me a - lone.
He prom - ised nev - er to leave me, Nev - er to leave me a - lone.
My Sav - ior whis-pered His prom - ise, Nev - er will leave me a - lone.
He prom - ised nev - er to leave me, Nev - er to leave me a - lone.

He prom - ised nev - er to leave me, Nev - er to leave me a - lone.

I'll Fly Away

ALBERT E. BRUMLEY

ALBERT E. BRUMLEY

1. Some glad morn-ing when this life is o'er,
2. When the shad-ows of this life have grown,
3. Just a few more wea - ry days and then,

I'll fly a - way; fly a - way fly a - way;

To a home on God's ce - les - tial shore,
Like a bird from pris - on bars has flown,
To a land where joys shall nev - er end,

I'll fly a - way. fly a - way, fly a - way.

I'll fly a - way, O glo - ry, I'll fly a - way;
fly a - way, fly a - way, in the morn - ing;

When I die, Hal - le - lu - jah, by and by, I'll fly a - way.
fly a - way, fly a - way.

The Love of God

FREDERICK M. LEHMAN

FREDERICK M. LEHMAN
Arranged by Claudia Lehman Mays

4

1. The love of God is great-er far Than tongue or pen can ev - er tell;
2. When hoar - y time shall pass a - way, And earth - ly thrones and king-doms fall,
3. Could we with ink the o - cean fill, And were the skies of parch-ment made.

It goes be - ond the high-est star, And reach-es to the low-est hell.
When men, who here re - fuse to pray, On rocks and hills and moun-tains call,
Were ev - 'ry stalk on earth a quill, And ev - 'ry man a scribe by trade,

The guilt - y pair, bowed down with care, God gave His Son to win;
God's love so pure, shall still en - dure, All mea - sure - less and strong;
To write the love of God a - bove Would drain the o - cean dry.

His err - ing child He rec - on - ciled, And par - doned from his sin.
Re - deem - ing grace to A - dam's race The saints' and an - gels' song.
Nor could the scroll con - tain the whole, Tho' stretched from sky to sky.

O love of God, how rich and pure! How mea-sure-less and strong!

It shall for-ev-er-more en-dure The saints' and an-gels' song.

Amazing Grace! How Sweet the Sound 5

St. 1-4, JOHN NEWTON
St. 5, Anonymous, c. 1790

Virginia Harmony, 1831
Arranged by Edwin O. Excell

1. A - maz - ing grace! how sweet the sound, That saved a wretch like me!
2. 'Twas grace that taught my heart to fear, And grace my fears re - lieved;
3. Thro' man - y dan - gers, toils, and snares, I have al - read - y come;
4. The Lord has prom - ised good to me, His word my hope se - cures;
5. When we've been there ten thou - sand years, Bright shin - ing as the sun,

I once was lost, but now am found, Was blind, but now I see.
How pre - cious did that grace ap - pear The hour I first be - lieved!
'Tis grace hath bro't me safe thus far, And grace will lead me home.
He will my shield and por - tion be As long as life en - dures.
We've no less days to sing God's praise Than when we first be - gun.

6 Precious Memories

J. B. F. WRIGHT

J. B. F. WRIGHT

1. Pre - cious mem-'ries,   un - seen an - gels,   Sent from some-where to   my soul;
2. Pre - cious fa - ther,   lov - ing moth- er,   Fly a - cross the lone - ly   years;
3. As   I   trav - el   on life's path-way,   Know not what the years may   hold;

How   they lin - ger,   ev - er near me,   And   the sa - cred past un - fold.
And   old home scenes   of   my child-hood,   In   fond mem - o - ry ap - pear.
As   I   pon - der,   hope grows fond-er,   Pre - cious mem-'ries flood my   soul.

Pre - cious mem-'ries,   how they lin - ger,   How   they ev - er flood my   soul;

In   the still - ness   of   the mid-night,   Pre - cious, sa - cred scenes un - fold.

He the Pearly Gates Will Open

FRED BLOM
Trans. by Nathaniel Carlson

ELSIE AHLWEN

1. Love di-vine, so great and won-drous, Deep and might-y, pure, sub-lime,
2. Like a dove when hunt-ed, fright-ened, As a wound-ed fawn was I;
3. Love di-vine, so great and won-drous, All my sins He then for-gave.
4. In life's e-ven-tide, at twi-light, At His door I'll knock and wait;

Com-ing from the heart of Je-sus, Just the same thro' tests of time!
Bro-ken-heart-ed, yet He healed me, He will heed the sin-ner's cry.
I will sing His praise for-ev-er, For His blood, His pow'r to save.
By the pre-cious love of Je-sus I shall en-ter heav-en's gate.

He the pear-ly gates will o-pen, So that I may en-ter in;

For He pur-chased my re-demp-tion And for-gave me all my sin.

Dwelling in Beulah Land

C. AUSTIN MILES

1. Far a-way the noise of strife up-on my ear is fall-ing,
2. Far be-low the storm of doubt up-on the world is beat-ing,
3. Let the storm-y breez-es blow, their cry can-not a-larm me,
4. View-ing here the works of God, I sink in con-tem-pla-tion,

Then I know the sins of earth be-set on ev-'ry hand;
Sons of men in bat-tle long the en-e-my with-stand;
I am safe-ly shel-ter'd here, pro-tect-ed by God's hand;
Hear-ing now His bless-ed voice, I see the way He planned;

Doubt and fear and things of earth in vain to me are call-ing,
Safe am I with-in the cas-tle of God's word re-treat-ing,
Here the sun is al-ways shin-ing, here there's naught can harm me,
Dwell-ing in the Spir-it, here I learn of full sal-va-tion,

None of these shall move me from Beu-lah Land.
Noth-ing there can reach me — 'tis Beu-lah Land.
I am safe for-ev-er in Beu-lah Land.
Glad-ly will I tar-ry in Beu-lah Land.

I'm liv-ing on the moun-tain, un-der-neath a cloud-less sky, I'm
Praise God!

drink- ing at the foun- tain that nev - er shall run dry, O yes! I'm feast- ing on the

man- na from a boun- ti- ful sup - ply For I am dwell- ing in Beu - lah Land.

HIS NAME IS WONDERFUL

udrey Mieir, composer and author, writes, "We were working in the Bethel Union Church, Duarte, California, where my husband's brother, Dr. Luther Mieir was pastor. Christmas was on Sunday, and we had made all the usual preparations that small churches make to present the Christmas story in its simplicity and beauty. The church was decorated with pine boughs. The choirloft had been converted into a manger scene, and we had chosen to use the young people to present the story. As the morning service began, I was almost overwhelmed with the fragrance, the sounds, and most of all, with the gentle moving of the Spirit in that church. The pastor stood to his feet, opened the Bible, and said, 'His name shall be called Wonderful.' I tell you the truth, that's all it took. I wrote words and music on the flyleaf of my Bible.

"In the Sunday evening service, I taught the chorus to a group of young people, and it was sung for the first time." (William J. Reynolds, reprinted from HANDBOOK TO *THE BAPTIST HYMNAL*)

10 Blessed Assurance, Jesus Is Mine

FANNY J. CROSBY

PHEOBE PALMER KNAPP

1. Bless-ed as - sur-ance, Je - sus is mine! Oh, what a fore-taste of glo - ry di - vine!
2. Per - fect sub - mis - sion, per-fect de-light, Vi-sions of rap-ture now burst on my sight:
3. Per - fect sub - mis - sion, all is at rest, I in my Sav - ior am hap-py and blest:

Heir of sal - va - tion, pur-chase of God, Born of His Spir - it, washed in His blood.
An - gels de - scend-ing bring from a - bove Ech - oes of mer - cy, whis-pers of love.
Watch-ing and wait - ing, look - ing a - bove, Filled with His good-ness, lost in His love.

This is my sto - ry, this is my song, Prais-ing my Sav - ior all the day long;

This is my sto - ry, this is my song, Prais-ing my Sav - ior all the day long.

The Unclouded Day

11

JOSIAH K. ALWOOD

JOSIAH K. ALWOOD

1. O they tell me of a home far be-yond the skies, O they tell me of a
2. O they tell me of a home where my friends have gone, O they tell me of a
3. O they tell me that He smiles on His chil-dren there, And His smile drives their

home far a-way; O they tell me of a home where no storm clouds rise,
land far a-way, Where the tree of life in e-ter-nal bloom
sor-rows all a-way, And they tell me that no tears ev-er come a-gain

O they tell me of an un-cloud-ed day.
Shed its fra-grance thro' the un-cloud-ed day. O the land of cloud-less day,
In that love-ly land of un-cloud-ed day.

O the land of an un-cloud-ed day; O they tell me of a

home where no storm clouds rise, O they tell me of an un-cloud-ed day.

12 Just Over in the Glory-Land

JAMES W. ACUFF

EMMETT S. DEAN

1. I've a home pre-pared where the saints a - bide, Just o - ver in the glo - ry - land;
2. I am on my way to those man-sions fair, Just o - ver in the glo - ry - land;
3. What a joy - ful tho't that my Lord I'll see, Just o - ver in the glo - ry - land;
4. With the blood-washed throng I will shout and sing, Just o - ver in the glo - ry - land;

And I long to be by my Sav - ior's side, Just o - ver in the glo - ry - land.
There to sing God's praise, and His glo - ry share, Just o - ver in the glo - ry - land.
And with kin - dred saved, there for - ev - er be, Just o - ver in the glo - ry - land.
Glad ho - san - nas to Christ, the Lord and King, Just o - ver in the glo - ry - land.

Just o - ver in the glo - ry - land, I'll join the hap - py an - gel band,
o - ver, o - ver yes, join

Just o - ver in the glo - ry - land; Just o - ver in the glo - ry - land,
o - ver, o - ver

There with the might - y host I'll stand, just o - ver in the glo - ry - land.
yes, with

Stepping in the Light

ELIZA E. HEWITT

WILLIAM J. KIRKPATRICK

13

1. Try - ing to walk in the steps of the Sav - ior, Try - ing to fol - low our
2. Press - ing more close - ly to Him who is lead - ing When we are tempt - ed to
3. Walk - ing in foot - steps of gen - tle for - bear - ance, Foot - steps of faith - ful - ness,
4. Try - ing to walk in the steps of the Sav - ior, Up - ward, still up - ward we'll

Sav - ior and King, Shap - ing our lives by His bless - ed ex - am - ple,
turn from the way, Trust - ing the arm that is strong to de - fend us,
mer - cy, and love, Look - ing to Him for the grace free - ly prom - ised,
fol - low our Guide; When we shall see Him, the King in His beau - ty,

Hap - py, how hap - py, the songs that we bring.
Hap - py, how hap - py, our prais - es each day.
Hap - py, how hap - py, our jour - ney a - bove.
Hap - py, how hap - py, our place at His side.

How beau - ti - ful to walk in the

steps of the Sav - ior, Step - ping in the light, step - ping in the light; How

beau - ti - ful to walk in the steps of the Sav - ior, Led in paths of light.

14 A New Name in Glory

C. AUSTIN MILES

C. AUSTIN MILES

1. I was once a sin-ner, but I came Par-don to re-ceive from my Lord:
2. I was hum-bly kneel-ing at the cross, Fear-ing naught but God's an-gry frown;
3. In the Book 'tis writ-ten "Saved by Grace," O the joy that came to my soul!

This was free-ly giv-en, and I found That He al-ways kept His word (kept His word).
When the heav-ens o-pened and I saw That my name was writ-ten down (writ-ten down).
Now I am for-giv-en and I know By the blood I am made whole (am made whole).

There's a new name writ-ten down in glo-ry, And it's mine, O yes, it's mine!
And it's mine, yes, it's mine!

And the white-robed an-gels sing the sto-ry, "A sin-ner has come home."

has come home.

For there's a new name writ-ten down in glo-ry, And it's mine, O yes, it's mine!
And it's mine, yes, it's mine!

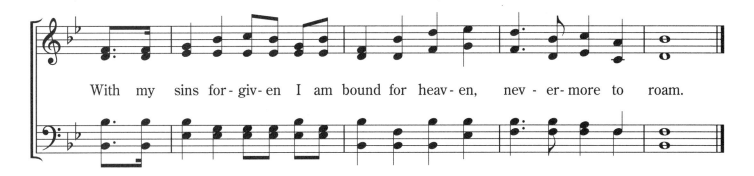

With my sins for-giv-en I am bound for heav-en, nev-er-more to roam.

WHEN THE ROLL IS CALLED UP YONDER

James M. Black writes: "While a teacher in a Sunday-school and president of a young people's society, ... I one day met a girl, fourteen years old, poorly clad and the child of a drunkard. She accepted my invitation to attend the Sunday-school, and joined the young people's society. One evening at a consecration-meeting, when members answered the roll-call by repeating Scripture texts, she failed to respond. I spoke of what a sad thing it would be, when our names are called from the Lamb's Book of Life, if one of us should be absent; and I said, 'O God, when my own name is called up yonder, may I be there to respond!' I longed for something suitable to sing just then, but I could find nothing in the books. We closed the meeting, and on my way home I was still wishing that there might be a song that could be sung on such occasions. The thought came to me, 'Why don't you make it? I dismissed the idea, thinking that I could never write such a hymn. When I reached my house my wife saw that I was deeply troubled, and questioned me, but I made no reply. Then the words of the first stanza came to me in full. In fifteen minutes more I had composed the other two verses. Going to the piano, I played the music just as it is found today in the hymn-books, note for note, and I have never dared to change a single word or a note of the piece since." (Hugh T. McElrath, reprinted from HANDBOOK TO *THE BAPTIST HYMNAL*) (Originally published in MY LIFE AND THE STORY OF THE GOSPEL HYMNS by Ira D. Sankey).

16 Trust and Obey

JOHN H. SAMMIS   DANIEL B. TOWNER

1. When we walk with the Lord In the light of His Word
2. Not a bur - den we bear, Not a sor - row we share,
3. But we nev - er can prove The de - lights of His love
4. Then in fel - low - ship sweet We will sit at His feet

What a glo - ry He sheds on our way! While we do His good will;
But our toil He doth rich - ly re - pay; Not a grief or a loss,
Un - til all on the al - tar we lay; For the fa - vor He shows
Or we'll walk by His side in the way; What He says we will do,

He a - bides with us still, And with all who will trust and o - bey.
No a frown or a cross, But is blest if we trust and o - bey.
And the joy He be - stows Are for them who will trust and o - bey.
Where He sends we will go, Nev - er fear, on - ly trust and o - bey.

Trust and o - bey, for there's no oth - er way To be

hap - py in Je - sus, But to trust and o - bey.

In Times Like These

RUTH CAYE JONES

RUTH CAYE JONES

18 A Mighty Fortress Is Our God

MARTIN LUTHER
Trans. Frederick H. Hedge

MARTIN LUTHER

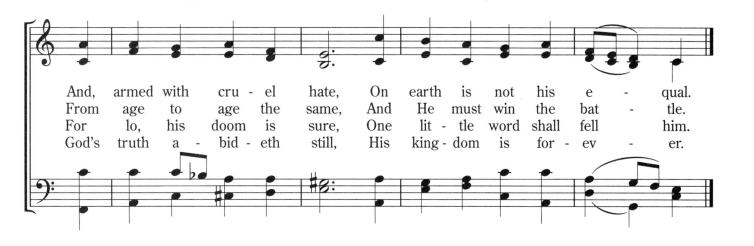

And, armed with cru-el hate, On earth is not his e - qual.
From age to age the same, And He must win the bat - tle.
For lo, his doom is sure, One lit-tle word shall fell him.
God's truth a - bid-eth still, His king-dom is for-ev - er.

Away in a Manger

19

St. 1, 2, Anonymous
St. 3, JOHN THOMAS McFARLAND

JAMES R. MURRAY

1. A - way in a man - ger, no crib for a bed, The lit - tle Lord
2. The cat - tle are low - ing, the Ba - by a - wakes, But lit - tle Lord
3. Be near me, Lord Je - sus, I ask Thee to stay Close by me for -

Je - sus laid down His sweet head; The stars in the sky looked
Je - sus, no cry - ing He makes; I love Thee, Lord Je - sus! look
ev - er, and love me, I pray; Bless all the dear chil - dren in

down where He lay, The lit - tle Lord Je - sus, a - sleep on the hay.
down from the sky, And stay by my cra - dle till morn - ing is nigh.
Thy ten - der care, And fit us for heav - en to live with Thee there.

20 Joy to the World! The Lord Is Come

ISAAC WATTS

GEORGE FREDERICK HANDEL
Arranged by Lowell Mason

1. Joy to the world! the Lord is come; Let earth re - ceive her
2. Joy to the earth! the Sav - ior reigns; Let men their songs em -
3. No more let sins and sor - rows grow, Nor thorns in - fest the
4. He rules the world with truth and grace, And makes the na - tions

King; Let ev - 'ry heart pre - pare Him room,
ploy; While fields and floods, rocks, hills, and plains
ground; He comes to make His bless - ings flow
prove The glo - ries of His righ - teous - ness,

And heav'n and na - ture sing, And heav'n and na - ture
Re - peat the sound - ing joy, Re - peat the sound - ing
Far as the curse is found, Far as the curse is
And won - ders of His love, And won - ders of His

1. And heav'n and na - ture sing,

1. And heav'n and na - ture sing, And

sing, And heav'n, and heav'n and na - ture sing.
joy, Re - peat, re - peat the sound - ing joy.
found, Far as, far as the curse is found.
love, And won - ders, won - ders of His love.

heav'n and na - ture sing,

O Come, All Ye Faithful

21

Latin Hymn
Ascribed to JOHN FRANCIS WADE
Trans. Frederick Oakeley and others

JOHN FRANCIS WADE

22   Silent Night, Holy Night

JOSEPH MOHR
Trans. st. 1, 3, John Freeman Young
Trans. st. 2, 4, Anonymous

FRANZ GRUBER

1. Si - lent night, ho - ly night, All is calm, all is bright Round yon
2. Si - lent night, ho - ly night, Dark - ness flies, all is light; Shep - herds
3. Si - lent night, ho - ly night, Son of God, love's pure light Ra - diant
4. Si - lent night, ho - ly night, Won - drous star, lend thy light; With the

vir - gin moth - er and child! Ho - ly In - fant so ten - der and mild,
hear the an - gels sing, "Al - le - lu - ia! hail the King!
beams from Thy ho - ly face, With the dawn of re - deem - ing grace,
an - gels let us sing Al - le - lu - ia to our King;

Sleep in heav - en - ly peace, Sleep in heav - en - ly peace.
Christ the Sav - ior is born, Christ the Sav - ior is born."
Je - sus, Lord, at Thy birth, Je - sus, Lord, at Thy birth.
Christ the Sav - ior is born, Christ the Sav - ior is born.

23   O Think of the Home Over There

DeWITT C. HUNTINGTON

TULLIUS C. O'KANE

1. O think of the home o - ver there, By the side of the riv - er of
2. O think of the friends o - ver there, Who be - fore us the jour - ney have
3. My Sav - ior is now o - ver there, There my kin - dred and friends are at
4. I'll soon be at home o - ver there, For the end of my jour - ney I

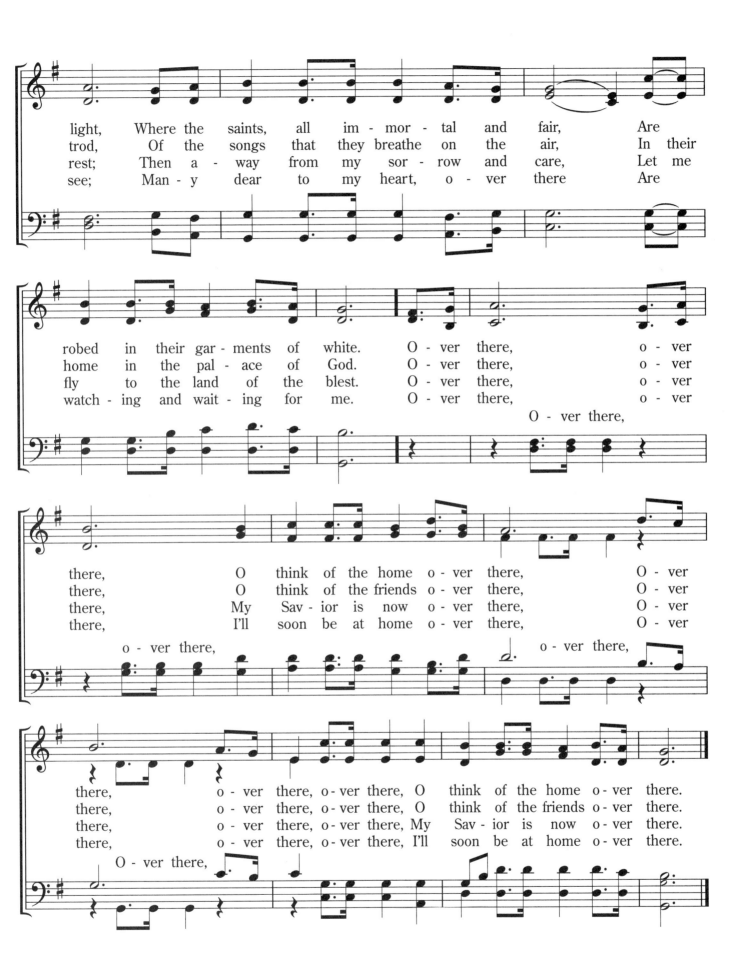

24   Kneel at the Cross

CHARLES E. MOODY   CHARLES E. MOODY

1. Kneel at the cross, Christ will meet you there, He in-ter-cedes for you;
2. Kneel at the cross, There is room for all Who would His glo-ry share;
3. Kneel at the cross, Give your i-dols up, Look un-to realms a-bove;

Lift up your voice, Leave with Him your care And be-gin life a-new.
Bliss there a-waits, Harm can ne'er be-fall Those who are an-chored there.
Turn not a-gain To life's spar-kling cup; Trust al-ways in His love.

Kneel at the cross, Leave ev-'ry care.
Kneel at the cross, Kneel at the cross, Leave ev-'ry care, Leave ev-'ry care;

Kneel at the cross, Je-sus will meet you there.
Kneel at the cross, Kneel at the cross, meet you there.

Bring Them In

ALEXCENAH THOMAS

WILLIAM A. OGDEN

1. Hark! 'Tis the Shep-herd's voice I hear, Out in the des-ert dark and drear,
2. Who'll go and help this Shep-herd kind, Help Him the wan-d'ring ones to find?
3. Out in the des-ert hear their cry, Out on the moun-tains wild and high,

Call - ing the sheep who've gone a-stray Far from the Shep-herd's fold a-way.
Who'll bring the lost ones to the fold, Where they'll be shel-tered from the cold?
Hark! 'Tis the Mas-ter speaks to thee, "Go find My sheep wher-e'er they be."

Bring them in, bring them in, Bring them in from the fields of sin;

Bring them in, bring them in, Bring the wan-d'ring ones to Je-sus.

26   Follow On

W. O. CUSHING

ROBERT LOWRY

1. Down in the val - ley with my Sav - ior I would go, Where the flow'rs are
2. Down in the val - ley with my Sav - ior I would go, Where the storms are
3. Down in the val - ley, or up - on the moun - tain steep, Close be - side my

bloom - ing and the sweet wa - ters flow; Ev - 'ry-where He leads me I would
sweep - ing and the dark wa - ters flow; With His hand to lead me I will
Sav - ior would my soul ev - er keep; He will lead me safe - ly in the

fol - low, fol - low on, Walk - ing in His foot-steps till the crown be won.
nev - er, nev - er fear, Dan - ger can - not fright me if my Lord is near.
path that He has trod, Up to where they gath - er on the hills of God.

Fol - low! fol - low! I would fol - low Je - sus! An - y-where, ev - 'ry-where, I would fol - low on!

Fol - low! fol - low! I would fol - low Je - sus! Ev - 'ry-where He leads me I would fol - low on!

Mansion Over the Hilltop

IRA F. STANPHILL

IRA F. STANPHILL

1. I'm sat-is-fied with just a cot-tage be-low, A lit-tle sil-ver
2. Tho' of-ten temp-ted, tor-ment-ed, and test-ed And like the proph-et
3. Don't think me poor or de-sert-ed or lone-ly, I'm not dis-cour-aged,

and a lit-tle gold; But in that cit-y where the ran-somed will shine,
my pil-low a stone; And tho' I find here no per-ma-nent dwell-ing,
I'm heav-en bound; I'm just a pil-grim in search of a cit-y,

I want a gold one that's sil-ver lined.
I know He'll give me a man-sion my own. I've got a man-sion just
I want a man-sion, a robe and a crown.

o-ver the hill-top, In that bright land where we'll nev-er grow old; And some day

yon-der we will nev-er more wan-der But walk the streets that are pur-est gold.

28 Majesty

JACK W. HAYFORD

JACK W. HAYFORD
Arranged by Eugene Thomas

Maj - es - ty, wor - ship His maj - es - ty;

Je - sus, who died, now glo - ri - fied, King of all kings.

MAJESTY

The words and music of this song were written by Jack W. Hayford in 1977. Hayford and his wife Anna were vacationing in Britain at the time. The author later wrote that the experience of visiting many of the castles of the land led him to: "Sense the influence one might feel if raised as a child in such regal settings... [It] became quite credible how a person used to such an environment might more likely conceive of themselves as being bred to influence their world.

"One day, as Anna and I drove along together, at once the opening lyrics and melody of 'Majesty' simply came to my heart. I continued driving, asking her to jot the words and the melody line in the notebook she had beside her."

The remainder of the song was written after the Hayfords returned to their home in California. (David W. Music, reprinted from HANDBOOK TO *THE BAPTIST HYMNAL*)

30 Under His Wings

WILLIAM O. CUSHING

IRA D. SANKEY

1. Un - der His wings I am safe - ly a - bid - ing, Tho' the night
2. Un - der His wings, what a ref - uge in sor - row! How the heart
3. Un - der His wings, O what pre - cious en - joy - ment! There will I

deep - ens and tem - pests are wild; Still I can trust Him, I
yearn - ing - ly turns to His rest! Of - ten when earth has no
hide till life's tri - als are o'er; Shel - tered, pro - tect - ed, no

know He will keep me, He has re - deemed me and I am His child.
balm for my heal - ing, There I find com - fort and there I am blessed.
e - vil can harm me, Rest - ing in Je - sus I'm safe ev - er - more.

Un - der His wings, un - der His wings, Who from His love can sev - er?

Un - der His wings my soul shall a - bide, Safe - ly a - bide for - ev - er.

Farther Along

J. R. BAXTER, Jr.

W. B. STEVENS

1. Tempt-ed and tried we're oft made to won-der Why it should be thus
2. When death has come and tak-en our loved ones, It leaves our home so
3. Faith-ful till death said our lov-ing Mas-ter, A few more days to
4. When we see Je-sus com-ing in glo-ry, When He comes from His

all the day long, While there are oth-ers liv-ing a-bout us.
lone-ly and drear; Then do we won-der why oth-ers pros-per,
la-bor and wait; Toils of the road will then seem as noth-ing,
home in the sky; Then we shall meet Him in that bright man-sion,

Nev-er mo-lest-ed tho' in the wrong.
Liv-ing so wick-ed year af-ter year.
As we sweep thro' the beau-ti-ful gate.
We'll un-der-stand it all by and by.

Far-ther a-long we'll

know all a-bout it, Far-ther a-long we'll un-der-stand why; Cheer up, my

broth-er, live in the sun-shine, We'll un-der-stand it all by and by.

32 Surely Goodness and Mercy

JOHN W. PETERSON
and ALFRED B. SMITH

JOHN W. PETERSON
and ALFRED B. SMITH

1. A pil - grim was I, and a - wan - d'ring, In the cold night of
2. He re - stor - eth my soul when I'm wea - ry, He giv - eth me
3. When I walk thro' the dark, lone - some val - ley, My Sav - ior will

sin I did roam, When Je - sus the kind Shep - herd
strength day by day; He leads me be - side the still
walk with me there; And safe - ly His great hand will

found me, And now I am on my way home.
wa - ters, He guards me each step of the way.
lead me To the man - sions He's gone to pre - pare.

Sure - ly good - ness and mer - cy shall fol - low me All the days

all the days of my life; Sure - ly good - ness and

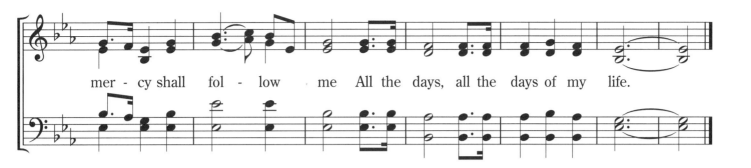

mer - cy shall fol - low me All the days, all the days of my life.

Beyond the Sunset

33

VIRGIL P. BROCK

BLANCHE KERR BROCK

1. Be - yond the sun - set, O bliss - ful morn - ing, When with our
2. Be - yond the sun - set, no clouds will gath - er, No storms will
3. Be - yond the sun - set, a hand will guide me To God, the
4. Be - yond the sun - set, O glad re - un - ion, With our dear

Sav - ior heav'n is be - gun. Earth's toil - ing end - ed, O glo - rious
threat - en, no fears an - noy; O day of glad - ness, O day un -
Fa - ther, whom I a - dore; His glo - rious pres - ence, His words of
loved ones who've gone be - fore; In that fair home - land we'll know no

dawn - ing; Be - yond the sun - set, when day is done.
end - ing, Be - yond the sun - set, e - ter - nal joy!
wel - come, Will be my por - tion on that fair shore.
part - ing, Be - yond the sun - set for - ev - er - more!

34   When They Ring the Golden Bells

DION DE MARBELLE   DION DE MARBELLE

1. There's a land be-yond the riv-er, That we call the sweet for-ev-er,
2. We shall know no sin or sor-row, In that ha-ven of to-mor-row,
3. When our days shall know their num-ber, And in death we sweet-ly slum-ber,

And we on-ly reach that shore by faith's de-cree; One by one we'll gain the por-tals,
When our barque shall sail be-yond the sil-ver sea; We shall on-ly know the bless-ing
When the King com-mands the spir-it to be free; Nev-er-more with an-guish la-den,

There to dwell with the im-mor-tals, When they ring the gol-den bells for you and me.
Of our Fa-ther's sweet ca-ress-ing, When they ring the gol-den bells for you and me.
We shall reach that love-ly ai-den, When they ring the gol-den bells for you and me.

(you and me).

Don't you hear the bells now ring-ing? Don't you hear the an-gels sing-ing? 'Tis the

glo - ry hal - le - lu - jah Ju - bi - lee. (Ju - bi-lee). In that far - off sweet for - ev - er,

Just be - yond the shin- ing riv- er, When they ring the gol-den bells for you and me.(you and me).

In the Garden

One day in March, 1912, C. Austin Miles was sitting in his home, in a combination study and photographic darkroom, reading the 20th chapter of John's gospel. It describes the arrival of Mary, Peter, and John at the tomb where Christ had been buried. As he read this account, in his imagination he saw all of this happening, heard the voices, and watched as a silent observer. From the inspiration of this experience, he remained at his desk and completed the words of the hymn. Later that evening he composed the music to "In the Garden." (William J. Reynolds, reprinted from HANDBOOK TO *THE BAPTIST HYMNAL*)

36 God Be with You

JEREMIAH E. RANKIN

WILLIAM G. TOMER

1. God be with you till we meet a-gain, By His coun-sels
2. God be with you till we meet a-gain, 'Neath His wings pro-
3. God be with you till we meet a-gain, When life's per-ils
4. God be with you till we meet a-gain, Keep love's ban-ner

guide, up-hold you, With His sheep se-cure-ly fold you,
tect-ing hide you, Dai-ly man-na still pro-vide you,
thick con-found you, Put His arms un-fail-ing round you,
float-ing o'er you; Smite death's threat-'ning wave be-fore you,

God be with you till we meet a-gain. Till we meet, till we

meet, Till we meet at Je-sus' feet, Till we
(till we meet,)

meet, till we meet, God be with you till we meet a-gain.

The Beautiful Garden of Prayer

ELEANOR ALLEN SCHROLL

J. H. FILLMORE

1. There's a gar-den where Je-sus is wait-ing, There's a place that is won-drous-ly fair; For it glows with the light of His pres-ence, 'Tis the beau-ti-ful gar-den of prayer.
2. There's a gar-den where Je-sus is wait-ing, And I go with my bur-den and care, Just to learn from His lips words of com-fort, In the beau-ti-ful gar-den of prayer.
3. There's a gar-den where Je-sus is wait-ing, And He bids you to come meet Him there; Just to bow and re-ceive a new bless-ing, In the beau-ti-ful gar-den of prayer.

O the beau-ti-ful gar-den, the gar-den of prayer, O the beau-ti-ful gar-den of prayer; There my Sav-ior a-waits, and He o-pens the gates To the beau-ti-ful gar-den of prayer.

38   'Neath the Old Olive Trees

B. B. McKINNEY   B. B. McKINNEY

1. 'Neath the stars of the night Walked the Sav - ior of light, In the gar - den of
2. All the sin of the world On the Sav - ior was hurled, As he knelt in the
3. May my song ev - er be Of the love prof - fered me, By my Lord all a -

dew - la - dened breeze; Where no light could be found, Je - sus knelt on the ground,
gar - den a - lone; Hear His soul - bur - dened plea, Let this cup pass from Me,
lone on His knees: Praise His won - der - ful name, he who bore all my blame,

There He prayed 'neath the old ol - ive trees.
"E - ven so, not My will, Thine be done." 'Neath the old ol - ive trees, 'Neath the
As He knelt 'neath the old ol - ive trees.

old ol - ive trees, Went the Sav - ior a - lone on His knees: "Not My will, Thine be

done," Cried the Fa - ther's own Son, As He knelt 'neath the old ol - ive trees.

The Old Rugged Cross

GEORGE BENNARD   GEORGE BENNARD

1. On a hill far a - way stood an old rug - ged cross, The em - blem of
2. Oh, that old rug - ged cross, so de - spised by the world, Has a won - drous at -
3. In the old rug - ged cross, stained with blood so di - vine, Such a won - der - ful
4. To the old rug - ged cross I will ev - er be true, Its shame and re -

suf - f'ring and shame; And I love that old cross where the dear - est and best
trac - tion for me; For the dear Lamb of God left His glo - ry a - bove,
beau - ty I see; For 'twas on that old cross Je - sus suf - fered and died,
proach glad - ly bear; Then He'll call me some day to my home far a - way,

For a world of lost sin - ners was slain.
To bear it to dark Cal - va - ry.   So I'll cher - ish the old rug - ged
To par - don and sanc - ti - fy me.
Where His glo - ry for - ev - er I'll share.

cross,   Till my tro - phies at last I lay down;   I will cling to the
old rug - ged cross,

old rug - ged cross,   And ex - change it some day for a crown.
cross,   the old rug - ged cross,

40 Bringing in the Sheaves

KNOWLES SHAW

GEORGE A. MINOR

1. Sow - ing in the morn - ing, sow - ing seeds of kind - ness, Sow - ing in the
2. Sow - ing in the sun - shine, sow - ing in the shad - ows, Fear - ing nei - ther
3. Go - ing forth with weep - ing, sow - ing for the Mas - ter, Tho' the loss sus -

noon - tide and the dew - y eve; Wait - ing for the har - vest,
clouds nor win - ter's chill - ing breeze; By and by the har - vest,
tained our spir - it of - ten grieves; When our weep - ing's o - ver,

and the time of reap - ing, We shall come re - joic - ing, bring - ing in the sheaves.
and the la - bor end - ed, We shall come re - joic - ing, bring - ing in the sheaves.
He will bid us wel - come, We shall come re - joic - ing, bring - ing in the sheaves.

Bring - ing in the sheaves, bring - ing in the sheaves, We shall come re - joic -

1 ing, bring - ing in the sheaves;

2 ing, bring - ing in the sheaves.

The Light of the World Is Jesus

PHILIP P. BLISS

41

PHILIP P. BLISS

42   How Great Thou Art

STUART K. HINE   STUART K. HINE

1. O Lord my God! When I in awe-some won-der Con-sid-er
2. When thro' the woods and for-est glades I wan-der, And hear the
3. And when I think that God, His Son not spar-ing, Sent Him to
4. When Christ shall come with shout of ac-cla-ma-tion, And take me

all the *worlds Thy hands have made, I see the stars, I hear the
birds sing sweet-ly in the trees; When I look down from loft-y
die, I scarce can take it in; That on the cross, my bur-den
home, what joy shall fill my heart! Then I shall bow in hum-ble

*roll-ing thun-der, Thy pow'r thro'-out the u-ni-verse dis-played.
moun-tain gran-deur, And hear the brook and feel the gen-tle breeze:
glad-ly bear-ing, He bled and died to take a-way my sin.
ad-o-ra-tion, And there pro-claim, my God, how great Thou art!

Then sings my soul, my Sav-ior God, to Thee;

* Author's original words are "works" and "mighty."

How great Thou art, how great Thou art! Then sings my soul, my

Sav - ior God, to Thee; How great Thou art, how great Thou art!

HEAVEN CAME DOWN

ohn W. Peterson writes, "This was written in the summer of 1961, when I was directing the singing one week at the Montrose Bible Conference in Montrose, Pennsylvania. During one of the sessions, an opportunity for personal testimony was given to the audience. An old gentleman rose to his feet and told of his conversion experience. In describing that night when he met Christ, he used the phrase, 'It seemed like heaven came down and glory filled my soul.' Right away I knew that it would be a fine title for a song, so I wrote it down and later in the week completed the song." (Harry Eskew, reprinted from HANDBOOK TO *THE BAPTIST HYMNAL*)

44 Each Step I Take

W. ELMO MERCER

W. ELMO MERCER

1. Each step I take my Sav-ior goes be - fore me, And with His lov-ing hand
2. At times I feel my faith be - gin to wa - ver, When up a - head I see
3. I trust in God, no mat - ter come what may, For life e - ter - nal

He leads the way. And with each breath I whis-per "I a - dore Thee;" Oh, what
a chas-m wide, It's then I turn and look up to my Sav - ior, I am
is in His hand, He holds the key that o - pens up the way, That will

joy to walk with Him each day.
strong when He is by my side. Each step I take I know that He will
lead me to the prom-ised land.

guide me; To high-er ground He ev-er leads me on. Un-til some day the last

step will be tak - en, Each step I take just leads me clos-er home.

The Banner of the Cross

45

DANIEL W. WHITTLE

JAMES McGRANAHAN

1. There's a roy-al ban-ner giv-en for dis-play To the sol-diers
2. Though the foe may rage and gath-er as the flood, Let the stan-dard
3. O - ver land and sea, wher-ev-er man may dwell, Make the glo-rious
4. When the glo-ry dawns — 'tis draw-ing ver-y near — It is hast'ning

of the King; As an en-sign fair we lift it up to-day,
be dis-played; And be-neath its folds, as sol-diers of the Lord,
ti-dings known; Of the crim-son ban-ner now the sto-ry tell,
day by day; Then be-fore our King the foe shall dis-ap-pear,

While as ran-somed ones we sing.
For the truth be not dis-mayed! March-ing on, march-ing
While the Lord shall claim His own! on, on,
And the cross the world shall sway!

on, For Christ count ev-'ry-thing but loss! And to
on, on, ev-'ry-thing, ev-'ry-thing but loss!

crown Him King, toil and sing 'Neath the ban-ner of the cross!
we'll Be - neath

46 Some Golden Daybreak

CARL BLACKMORE

CARL BLACKMORE

Will There Be Any Stars

ELIZA E. HEWITT

JOHN R. SWENEY

1. I am think-ing to-day of that beau-ti-ful land I shall reach when the sun go-eth down; When thro' won-der-ful grace by my Sav-ior I stand, Will there be an-y stars in my crown?

2. In the strength of the Lord let me la-bor and pray, Let me watch as a win-ner of souls, That bright stars may be mine in the glo-ri-ous day, When His praise like the sea bil-low rolls. Will there be an-y stars, an-y stars in my crown

3. Oh, what joy it will be when His face I be-hold, Liv-ing gems at His feet to lay down; It would sweet-en my bliss in the cit-y of gold, Should there be an-y stars in my crown.

When at eve-ning the sun go-eth down? When I wake with the blest In the man-sions of rest, Will there be an-y stars in my crown?

48 Victory in Jesus

E. M. BARTLETT

E. M. BARTLETT

1. I heard an old, old sto-ry, how a Sav-ior came from glo-ry,
2. I heard a-bout His heal-ing, of his cleans-ing pow'r re-veal-ing,
3. I heard a-bout a man-sion He has built for me in glo-ry,

How He gave His life on Cal-va-ry to save a wretch like me:
How He made the lame to walk a-gain and caused the blind to see;
And I heard a-bout the streets of gold be-yond the crys-tal sea;

I heard a-bout His groan-ing, of His pre-cious blood's a-ton-ing,
And then I cried, "Dear Je-sus, come and heal my bro-ken spir-it,"
A-bout the an-gels sing-ing, and the old re-demp-tion sto-ry,

Then I re-pent-ed of my sins and won the vic-to-ry.
And some-how Je-sus came and bro't to me the vic-to-ry.
And some sweet day I'll sing up there the song of vic-to-ry.

O vic-to-ry in Je-sus, my Sav-ior, for-ev-er, He sought me and bo't me with His re-deem-ing blood; He loved me ere I knew Him, and all my love is due Him, He plunged me to vic-to-ry, be-neath the cleans-ing flood.

Lord, Send a Revival

49

B. B. McKINNEY

B. B. McKINNEY

Lord, send a re-viv-al, Lord, send a re-viv-al, Lord, send a re-viv-al, And let it be-gin in me.

50 His Eye Is on the Sparrow

CIVILLA D. MARTIN

CHARLES H. GABRIEL

1. Why should I feel dis-cour-aged? Why should the shad-ows come?
2. "Let not your heart be trou-bled," His ten-der word I hear;
3. When-ev-er I am tempt-ed, When-ev-er clouds a-rise,

Why should my heart be lone-ly And long for heav'n and home
And rest-ing on His good-ness, I lose my doubt and fears;
When song gives place to sigh-ing, When hope with-in me dies,

When Je-sus is my por-tion? My con-stant Friend is He:
Tho' by the path He lead-eth, But one step I may see:
I draw the clos-er to Him; From care He sets me free:

His eye is on the spar-row, And I know He watch-es me.
His eye is on the spar-row, And I know He watch-es me.
His eye is on the spar-row, And I know He watch-es me.

His eye is on the spar - row, And I know He watch - es me.
His eye is on the spar - row, And I know He watch - es me.
His eye is on the spar - row, And I know He watch - es me.

I sing be - cause I'm hap - py, I sing be - cause I'm free;
I'm hap - py, I'm free;

For His eye is on the spar - row, And I know He watch - es me.

Sweeter As the Years Go By

51

LELIA N. MORRIS   LELIA N. MORRIS

Sweet - er as the years go by, Sweet - er as the years go by;
Sweet - er as the years go by, 'tis Sweet - er as the years go by;

Rich - er, full - er, deep - er, Je - sus' love is sweet - er, Sweet - er as the years go by.

52 When the Roll Is Called Up Yonder

JAMES M. BLACK   JAMES M. BLACK

roll   is called up yon - der, When the roll   is

When the roll is called up yon-der, I'll be there,   When the roll is

called up yon - der, When the roll is called up yon-der, I'll be there.

HARMONY WITH GOD

Music can feed the soul like food feeds the body! The blending harmony of an orchestra can lift us to realms of splendor. Harmony requires the combination of simultaneous musical notes in a chord. If an instrument is off pitch, the harmony is lost.

We are much like musical instruments in the hand of God. If our lives are in tune with his will, harmony results, and God is pleased with the music of our souls. We do blend in concert with others to produce beautiful harmony and praise.

This scene is seen in 2 Chronicles 5:13, "The trumpeters and singers were as one, to make one sound to be heard in praising and thanking the Lord; and when they lifted their voice with the trumpets and cymbals and instruments of music, and praised the Lord..." (Ruth Stallings, reprinted from MATURE LIVING)

54 No, Not One

JOHNSON OATMAN, Jr.   GEORGE C. HUGG

1. There's not a friend like the low-ly Je-sus, No, not one! No, not one!
2. No friend like Him is so high and ho-ly, No, not one! No, not one!
3. There's not an hour that He is not near us, No, not one! No, not one!
4. Did ev-er saint find this friend for-sake Him? No, not one! No, not one!
5. Was e'er a gift like the Sav-ior giv-en? No, not one! No, not one!

None else could heal all our soul's dis-eas-es, No, not one! No, not one!
And yet no friend is so meek and low-ly, No, not one! No, not one!
No night so dark but His love can cheer us, No, not one! No, not one!
Or sin-ner find that He would not take him? No, not one! No, not one!
Will He re-fuse us a home in heav-en? No, not one! No, not one!

Je-sus knows all a-bout our strug-gles, He will guide till the day is done;

There's not a friend like the low-ly Je-sus, No, not one! No, not one!

"Are Ye Able," Said the Master

EARL MARLATT

HARRY S. MASON

56 Some Day the Silver Cord Will Break

FANNY J. CROSBY

GEORGE C. STEBBINS

1. Some day the sil-ver cord will break, And I no more as now shall sing;
2. Some day my earth-ly house will fall — I can-not tell how soon 'twill be,
3. Some day, when fades the gold-en sun Be-neath the ro-sy-tint-ed west,
4. Some day — till then I'll watch and wait, My lamp all trimmed and burn-ing bright,

But O the joy when I shall wake With-in the pal-ace of the King!
But this I know: may All in All Has now a place in heav'n for me.
My bless-ed Lord will say, "Well done!" And I shall en-ter in-to rest.
That when my Sav-ior opens the gate, My soul to Him may take its flight.

And I shall see Him face to face, And tell the sto-ry saved by grace;
shall see to face,

And I shall see Him face to face, And tell the sto-ry saved by grace.
shall see to face,

Sweet Peace, the Gift of God's Love

PETER P. BILHORN

PETER P. BILHORN

57

1. There comes to my heart one sweet strain (sweet strain), A glad and a joy-ous re-frain (re-frain); I sing it a-gain and a-gain, Sweet peace, the gift of God's love.

2. Thro' Christ on the cross peace was made (was made), My debt by His death was all paid (all paid); No oth-er foun-da-tion is laid For peace, the gift of God's love.

3. In Je-sus for peace I a-bide (a-bide), And as I keep close to His side (His side), There's noth-ing but peace doth be-tide, Sweet peace, the gift of God's love.

Peace, peace, sweet peace! Won-der-ful gift from a-bove (a-bove)! Oh, won-der-ful, won-der-ful peace! Sweet peace, the gift of God's love!

58 Heaven Came Down

JOHN W. PETERSON

JOHN W. PETERSON

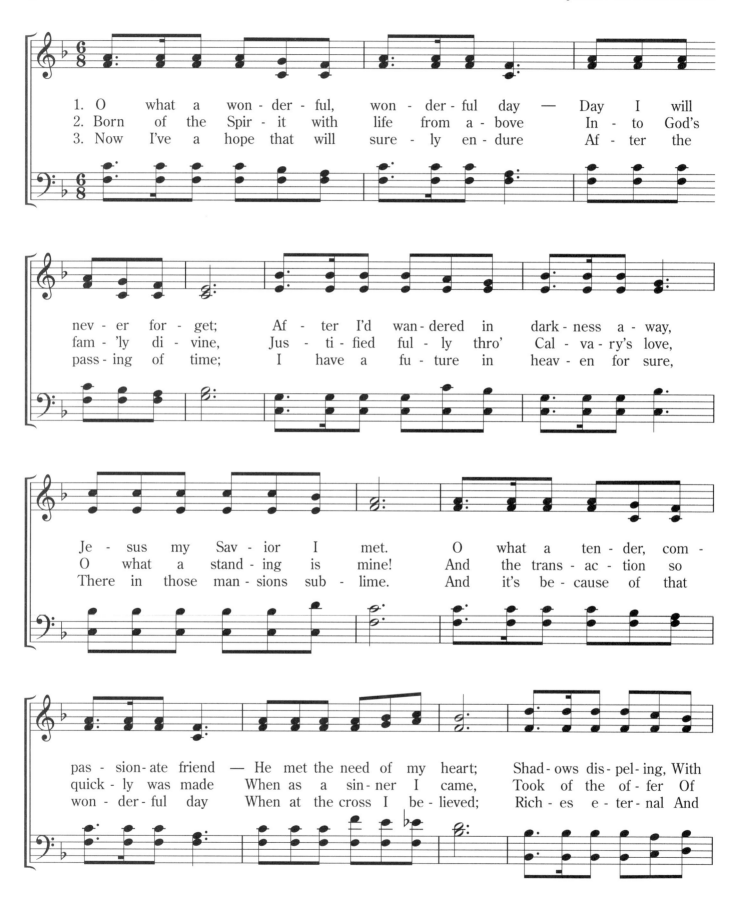

1. O what a won-der-ful, won-der-ful day — Day I will never for-get; After I'd wan-dered in dark-ness a-way, Je-sus my Sav-ior I met. O what a ten-der, com-pas-sion-ate friend — He met the need of my heart; Shad-ows dis-pel-ing, With

2. Born of the Spir-it with life from a-bove In-to God's fam-'ly di-vine, Jus-ti-fied ful-ly thro' Cal-va-ry's love, O what a stand-ing is mine! And the trans-ac-tion so quick-ly was made When as a sin-ner I came, Took of the of-fer Of

3. Now I've a hope that will sure-ly en-dure Af-ter the pass-ing of time; I have a fu-ture in heav-en for sure, There in those man-sions sub-lime. And it's be-cause of that won-der-ful day When at the cross I be-lieved; Rich-es e-ter-nal And

joy I am tell - ing, He made all the dark - ness de - part!
grace He did prof - fer He saved me, O praise His dear name!
bless - ings su - per - nal From His pre - cious hand I re - ceived.

Heav - en came down and glo - ry filled my soul, (filled my soul,)

When at the cross the Sav - ior made me whole; (made me whole;) My

sins were washed a - way — And my night was turned to day —

Heav - en came down and glo - ry filled my soul! (filled my soul!)

59 Work, for the Night Is Coming

ANNIE L. COGHILL   LOWELL MASON

1. Work, for the night is com - ing, Work thro' the morn - ing hours;
2. Work, for the night is com - ing, Work in the sun - ny noon;
3. Work, for the night is com - ing, Un - der the sun - set skies;

Work while the dew is spar - kling, Work 'mid spring - ing flow'rs:
Fill bright - est hours with la - bor, Rest comes sure and soon:
While their bright tints are glow - ing, Work, for day - light flies:

Work when the day grows bright - er, Work in the glow - ing sun;
Give ev - 'ry fly - ing min - ute Some - thing to keep in store;
Work till the last beam fad - eth, Fad - eth to shine no more;

Work, for the night is com - ing, When man's work is done.
Work, for the night is com - ing, When man works no more.
Work, for the night is dark - 'ning, When man's work is o'er.

My God and I

60

AUSTRIS A. WIHTOL

AUSTRIS A. WIHTOL

1. My God and I go in the field to-geth-er, We walk and
2. He tells me of the years that went be-fore me, When heav'n-ly
3. My God and I will go for aye to-geth-er, We'll walk and

talk as good friends should and do; We clasp our hands, our
plans were made for me to be, When all was but a
talk as good friends should and do; This earth will pass, and

voic-es ring with laugh-ter, My God and I walk thro' the mead-ow's
dream of dim con-cep-tion, To come to life, earth's ver-dant glo-ry
with it com-mon tri-fles, But God and I will go un-end-ing-

hue; We clasp our hands, our voic-es ring with laugh-ter,
see; When all was but a dream of dim con-cep-tion,
ly; This earth will pass, and with it com-mon tri-fles,

My God and I walk through the mead-ow's hue.
To come to life, earth's ver-dant glo-ry see.
But God and I will go un-end-ing-ly.

61

Because He Lives

GLORIA GAITHER
and WILLIAM J. GAITHER

WILLIAM J. GAITHER

1. God sent His Son, they called Him Je - sus; He came to love,
2. How sweet to hold a new-born ba - by, And feel the pride,
3. And then one day I'll cross the riv - er; I'll fight life's fi -

heal, and for - give; He lived and died to buy my
and joy He gives; But great - er still the calm as -
nal war with pain; And then as death gives way to

par - don, An emp - ty grave is there to prove my Sav - ior lives.
sur - ance, This child can face un - cer - tain days be - cause He lives.
vic - t'ry, I'll see the lights of glo - ry and I'll know He lives.

Be - cause He lives I can face to - mor - row; Be - cause He

lives all fear is gone; Be - cause I know He holds the

fu - ture, And life is worth the liv - ing just be - cause He lives.

For God So Loved the World 62

FRANCES TOWNSEND

ALFRED B. SMITH

For God so loved the world He gave His on - ly Son To die on Cal-v'ry's tree, From sin to set me free; Some day He's com - ing back — What glo - ry that will be! Won - der - ful His love to me.

63 Thank You, Lord

SETH SYKES
and BESSIE SYKES

SETH SYKES
and BESSIE SYKES

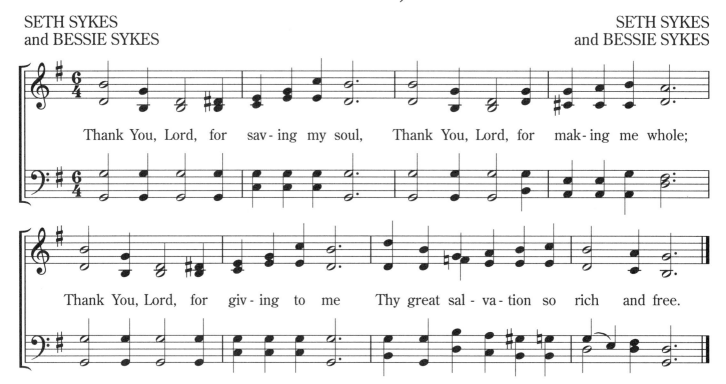

Thank You, Lord, for sav-ing my soul, Thank You, Lord, for mak-ing me whole;

Thank You, Lord, for giv-ing to me Thy great sal-va-tion so rich and free.

64 Tell Me the Old, Old Story

KATHERINE HANKEY

WILLIAM H. DOANE

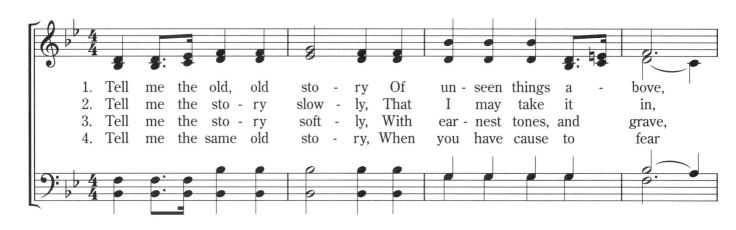

1. Tell me the old, old sto - ry Of un - seen things a - bove,
2. Tell me the sto - ry slow - ly, That I may take it in,
3. Tell me the sto - ry soft - ly, With ear - nest tones, and grave,
4. Tell me the same old sto - ry, When you have cause to fear

65 Great Is Thy Faithfulness

THOMAS O. CHISHOLM

WILLIAM M. RUNYAN

hand hath pro-vid-ed; Great is Thy faith-ful-ness, Lord, un-to me!

HIS EYE IS ON THE SPARROW

Ethel Waters often sang this song for the Billy Graham Crusades. Years before she had made the song famous by singing it in a Broadway play (later made into a movie), *The Member of the Wedding*. Originally, her part in the play didn't include "His Eye Is on the Sparrow." She was to sing a Russian lullaby to the young girl in the story. That didn't seem natural to Ethel—for her character, an old black cook from Georgia, to sing a Russian song. When she asked Carson McCullers, the author of the play, about it, Carson asked, "What song would you sing?"

Ethel started to sing "Sparrow" with all the tenderness and yearning she possessed. When she finished singing, the young, brilliant author had her head in Ethel's lap, crying.

Ethel had first heard that song as a child when her grandmother sang it to her, along with many others. Her grandmother had been the only one who tried to give Ethel some stability and moral direction during her childhood in Philadelphia. As a 12-year-old, she attended a revival and trusted Jesus as her Savior. Throughout her life, Ethel had tried to remember that God's eye was watching over her, but there were many times when she felt drowned in discouragement and loneliness.

Her success in several Broadway shows and movies had done little to ease the unfulfilled hunger inside her. She had been through two unsuccessful marriages, and she was childless. Often, she would give her one-woman shows on Broadway to standing ovations and repeated curtain calls, only to go back to an empty hotel room and cry herself to sleep. She knew that she was missing something, something that the cornhusks of the world could not take the place of.

The first Billy Graham Crusade that Ethel attended was in the 50's at Madison Square Garden, New York City. She began singing in the choir every night. One night during a rehearsal, Cliff Barrows asked her if she would sing "Sparrow" the next week. Almost reluctantly, she said, yes. She knew she was facing a decision. Would she go on trying to "straddle the fence" with her Christian life, or would she give all of her talent and her life to God? The night she sang "Sparrow," she decided that no matter what, she would sing only for her Lord. And so she did. For the rest of her life, she sang for the Crusades whenever her health permitted. If she had a spot on a TV variety show, she sang a gospel song.

It wasn't until this period of her life that she began to feel that she truly had found a home—in God's house with God's people. Then she could say, "I know I'm the sparrow He's watched over all these years."

"Yea, the sparrow hath found an house, and the swallow a nest for herself, where she may lay her young, even thine altars, O Lord of hosts, my King, and my God. Blessed are they that dwell in thy house: they will still be praising thee" (Ps. 84:3-4). (Reprinted from THE CHURCH MUSICIAN)

67 In My Heart There Rings a Melody

ELTON M. ROTH

ELTON M. ROTH

Beautiful Isle of Somewhere

J. S. FEARIS   J. S. FEARIS

69 When I See the Blood

JOHN G. FOOTE

JOHN G. FOOTE

1. Christ our Re-deem-er died on the cross, Died for the sin-ner,
2. Chief-est of sin-ners, Je-sus can save. As He has prom-ised,
3. Judg-ment is com-ing, all will be there. Who have re-ject-ed,
4. Oh, what com-pas-sion, oh, bound-less love! Je-sus hath pow-er,

paid all his due; All who re-ceive Him need nev-er fear,
so will He do; Oh sin-ner, hear Him, trust in His Word,
who have re-fused? Oh, sin-ner, has-ten, let Je-sus in,
Je - sus is true; All who be-lieve are safe from the storm,

Yes, He will pass, will pass o - ver you.
Then He will pass, will pass o - ver you.
Then God will pass, will pass o - ver you.
Oh, He will pass, will pass o - ver you. When I see the

When I

blood, When I see the blood, When I see the
see the blood, When I see the blood, When I

blood, I will pass, I will pass o - ver you.
see the blood, o - ver you.

When We All Get to Heaven

ELIZA E. HEWITT

EMILY D. WILSON

71 Does Jesus Care?

FRANK E. GRAEFF

J. LINCOLN HALL

1. Does Je - sus care when my heart is pained Too deep - ly for mirth or song,
2. Does Je - sus care when my way is dark With a name - less dread and fear?
3. Does Je - sus care when I've tried and failed To re - sist some temp - ta - tion strong;
4. Does Je - sus care when I've said "good-bye" To the dear - est on earth to me,

As the bur - dens press, And the cares dis - tress, And the way grows wea - ry and long?
As the day - light fades In - to deep night shades, Does He care e - nough to be near?
When for my deep grief There is no re - lief, Tho' my tears flow all the night long?
And my sad heart aches Till it near - ly breaks, Is it aught to Him? does He see?

O yes, He cares, I know He cares, His heart is touched with my grief;

When the days are wea - ry, The long night drea - ry, I know my Sav - ior cares. (He cares).

Ivory Palaces

HENRY BARRACLOUGH   HENRY BARRACLOUGH

1. My Lord has gar-ments so won-drous fine, And myrrh their tex-ture fills;
2. His life had al-so its sor-rows sore, For al-oes had a part;
3. His gar-ments too were in cas-sia dipped, With heal-ing in a touch;
4. In gar-ments glo-ri-ous He will come, To o-pen wide the door;

Its fra-grance reached to this heart of mine, With joy my be-ing thrills.
And when I think of the cross He bore, My eyes with tear-drops start.
Each time my feet in some sin have slipped, He took me from its clutch.
And I shall en-ter my heav'n-ly home, To dwell for-ev-er-more.

(mel.)
Out of the i-vo-ry pal-a-ces, In-to a world of woe,

(mel.)
On-ly His great, e-ter-nal love Made my Sav-ior go.

73 This World Is Not My Home

Arr. Albert E. Brumley

1. This world is not my home, I'm just a-pass-ing thro'. My trea-sures
2. They're all ex-pect-ing me, and that's one thing I know. My Sav-ior
3. I have a lov-ing Sav-ior up in glo-ry-land, I don't ex-
4. Just up in glo-ry-land we'll live e-ter-nal-ly, The saints on

are laid up some-where be-yond the blue; The an-gels beck-on me from
par-doned me and now I on-ward go; I know He'll take me thro' though
pect to stop un-til I with Him stand, He's wait-ing now for me in
ev-'ry hand are shout-ing vic-to-ry; Their songs of sweet-est praise drift

heav-en's o-pen door, And I can't feel at home in this world an-y-more.
I am weak and poor, And I can't feel at home in this world an-y-more.
heav-en's o-pen door, And I can't feel at home in this world an-y-more.
back from heav-en's shore, And I can't feel at home in this world an-y-more.

O Lord, you know I have no friend like You; If heav-en's not my home, then

Lord, what will I do? The an-gels beck-on me from heav-en's o-pen door,

And I can't feel at home in this world an-y-more.

AT CALVARY

The words had been vaguely in Willam R. Newell's mind for a few weeks and then, one day, on his way to lecture, they suddenly began crystallizing in his mind. He stepped into an unoccupied classroom and wrote them down quickly on the back of an envelope as they now appear. Proceeding to his class, he met Daniel B. Towner, then director of music at Moody Bible Institute, handed him the verses and suggested that he compose suitable music for them. When the author returned from his class, Dr. Towner had completed the tune, and they sang it together. (William J. Reynolds, reprinted from HANDBOOK TO *THE BAPTIST HYMNAL*)

75 Wonderful Peace

W. D. CORNELL, alt.

W. G. COOPER

1. Far a - way in the depths of my spir - it to - night Rolls a
2. What a trea - sure I have in this won - der - ful peace, Bur - ied
3. I am rest - ing to - night in this won - der - ful peace, Rest - ing
4. And me - thinks when I rise to that cit - y of peace, Where the
5. Ah, soul! are you here with - out com - fort and rest, March - ing

mel - o - dy sweet - er than psalm; In ce - les - tial - like strains it un -
deep in the heart of my soul, So se - cure that no pow - er can
sweet - ly in Je - sus' con - trol; For I'm kept from all dan - ger by
Au - thor of peace I shall see, That one strain of the song which the
down the rough path - way of time? Make Je - sus your Friend ere the

ceas - ing - ly falls O'er my soul like an in - fi - nite calm.
mine it a - way, While the years of e - ter - ni - ty roll!
night and by day, And His glo - ry is flood - ing my soul!
ran - somed will sing In that heav - en - ly king - dom will be:
shad - ows grow dark; O ac - cept of this peace so sub - lime!

Peace, peace, won - der - ful peace, Com - ing down from the Fa - ther a - bove! Sweep

o - ver my spir - it for - ev - er, I pray, In fath - om - less bil - lows of love!

The Longer I Serve Him

WILLIAM J. GAITHER   WILLIAM J. GAITHER

1. Since I start-ed for the king-dom, Since my life He con-
2. Ev-'ry need He is sup-ply-ing, Plen-teous grace He be-

trols, Since I gave my heart to Je-sus, The lon-ger I
stows; Ev-'ry day my way gets bright-er, The lon-ger I

serve Him, the sweet-er He grows.
serve Him, the sweet-er He grows. The lon-ger I serve Him the sweet-er He

grows, The more that I love Him, more love He be-stows; Each day is like

heav-en, my heart o-ver-flows, The lon-ger I serve Him, the sweet-er He grows.

77 His Name Is Wonderful

AUDREY MIEIR

AUDREY MIEIR

Be Still, My Soul

KATHARINA VON SCHLEGEL
Trans. by Jane L. Borthwick

JEAN SIBELIUS

1. Be still, my soul! the Lord is on thy side; Bear patient-
2. Be still, my soul! thy God doth undertake To guide the
3. Be still, my soul! the hour is hast'ning on When we shall

ly the cross of grief or pain. Leave to thy God to
future as He has the past. Thy hope, thy confi-
be forever with the Lord, When disappointment,

order and provide; In ev'ry change He faithful will re-
dence let nothing shake; All now mysterious shall be bright at
grief, and fear are gone, Sorrow forgot, love's purest joys re-

main. Be still, my soul! thy best, thy heav'nly Friend
last. Be still, my soul! the waves and winds still know
stored. Be still, my soul! when change and tears are past,

Thro' thorny ways leads to a joyful end.
His voice who ruled them while He dwelt below.
All safe and blessed we shall meet at last.

79 A Shelter in the Time of Storm

VERNON J. CHARLESWORTH

IRA D. SANKEY

1. The Lord's our Rock, in Him we hide, A shel-ter in the time of storm;
2. A shade by day, de-fense by night, A shel-ter in the time of storm;
3. The rag-ing storms may round us beat, A shel-ter in the time of storm;
4. O Rock di-vine, O Ref-uge dear, A shel-ter in the time of storm;

Se - cure what-ev-er ill be-tide, A shel-ter in the time of storm.
No fears a-larm, no foes af-fright, A shel-ter in the time of storm.
We'll nev-er leave our safe re-treat, A shel-ter in the time of storm.
Be Thou our help-er ev-er near, A shel-ter in the time of storm.

Oh, Je-sus is a Rock in a wea-ry land, A wea-ry land, a wea-ry land;

Oh, Je-sus is a Rock in a wea-ry land, A shel-ter in the time of storm.

In the Garden

C. AUSTIN MILES

C. AUSTIN MILES

1. I come to the gar-den a-lone, While the dew is still on the ros-es; And the voice I hear, fall-ing on my ear, The Son of God dis-clos-es.

2. He speaks, and the sound of His voice Is so sweet the birds hush their sing-ing; And the mel-o-dy that He gave to me With-in my heart is ring-ing.

3. I'd stay in the gar-den with Him Tho' the night a-round me be fall-ing; But He bids me go; thro' the voice of woe, His voice to me is call-ing.

And He walks with me, and He talks with me, And He tells me I am His own, And the joy we share as we tar-ry there, None oth-er has ev-er known.

81 It Is Well with My Soul

HORATIO G. SPAFFORD

PHILIP P. BLISS

1. When peace, like a riv - er, at - tend - eth my way, When
2. Tho' Sa - tan should buf - fet, tho' tri - als should come, Let
3. My sin — oh, the bliss of this glo - ri - ous tho't: My
4. And, Lord, haste the day when the faith shall be sight, The

sor - rows like sea bil - lows roll; What - ev - er my lot, Thou hast
this blest as - sur - ance con - trol, That Christ has re - gard - ed my
sin not in part, but the whole Is nailed to the cross and I
clouds be rolled back as a scroll, The trump shall re - sound and the

taught me to say, It is well, it is well with my soul.
help - less es - tate, And hath shed His own blood for my soul.
bear it no more, Praise the Lord, praise the Lord, O my soul!
Lord shall de - scend, "E - ven so," it is well with my soul.

It is well with my soul, It is well, it is well with my soul.
It is well with my soul,

O Say, but I'm Glad

82

Rev. JAMES P. SULLIVAN

MILDRED ELLEN SULLIVAN

1. There is a song in my heart to-day, Some-thing I nev-er had;
2. Won-der-ful, mar-vel-ous love He brings, In-to a heart that's sad;
3. Won't you come to Him with all your care, Wea-ry and worn and sad?

Je - sus has tak - en my sins a - way, O say, but I'm glad!
Thro' dark - est tun - nels the soul just sings, O say, but I'm glad!
You, too, will sing as His love you share, O say, but I'm glad!

O say, but I'm glad, I'm glad, O say, but I'm glad!

Je - sus has come and my cup's o - ver-run, O say, but I'm glad!

83
Anywhere with Jesus

JESSIE BROWN POUNDS
Adapted by Helen C. Dixon

DANIEL B. TOWNER

1. An - y - where with Je - sus I can safe - ly go,
2. An - y - where with Je - sus I am not a - lone;
3. An - y - where with Je - sus, o - ver land and sea,
4. An - y - where with Je - sus I can go to sleep,

An - y - where He leads me in this world be - low;
Oth - er friends may fail me, He is still my own;
Tell - ing souls in dark - ness of sal - va - tion free;
When the dark - 'ning shad - ows round a - bout me creep,

An - y - where with - out Him dear - est joys would fade;
Tho' His hand may lead me o - ver drear - est ways,
Read - y as He sum - mons me to go or stay,
Know - ing I shall wak - en nev - er - more to roam;

An - y - where with Je - sus I am not a - fraid.
An - y - where with Je - sus is a house of praise.
An - y - where with Je - sus when He points the way.
An - y - where with Je - sus will be home, sweet home.

An - y-where, an - y-where! Fear I can - not know;

An - y-where with Je - sus I can safe - ly go.

To God Be the Glory

"To God Be the Glory" is one of the finest hymns to come from the combined work of Fanny J. Crosby and William M. Doane. It was written by the blind poet in 1875 and was submitted to Doane who first published it.

The hymn was little known in this country until it was used by Cliff Barrows in the Nashville Billy Graham Crusade in 1954. Since then it has become immensely popular. (Hugh T. McElrath, reprinted from HAND-BOOK TO *THE BAPTIST HYMNAL*)

85 His Way with Thee

CYRUS S. NUSBAUM

What a Friend We Have in Jesus

JOSEPH SCRIVEN

CHARLES C. CONVERSE

86

1. What a friend we have in Jesus, All our sins and griefs to bear!
2. Have we trials and temptations? Is there trouble anywhere?
3. Are we weak and heavy laden, Cumbered with a load of care?

What a privilege to carry Ev'rything to God in prayer!
We should never be discouraged, Take it to the Lord in prayer:
Precious Savior, still our refuge; Take it to the Lord in prayer:

Oh, what peace we often forfeit, Oh, what needless pain we bear,
Can we find a friend so faithful Who will all our sorrows share?
Do thy friends despise, forsake thee? Take it to the Lord in prayer;

All because we do not carry Ev'rything to God in prayer!
Jesus knows our ev'ry weakness, Take it to the Lord in prayer.
In His arms He'll take and shield thee; Thou wilt find a solace there.

87 I Walk with the King

JAMES ROWE

B. D. ACKLEY

1. In sor-row I wan-dered, my spir-it op-pressed, But now I am
2. For years in the fet-ters of sin I was bound, The world could not
3. O soul near de-spair in the low-lands of strife, Look up and let

hap-py — se-cure-ly I rest; From morn-ing till ev-'ning glad
help me — no com-fort I found; But now like the birds and the
Je-sus come in-to your life; The joy of sal-va-tion to

car-ols I sing, And this is the rea-son: I walk with the King.
sun-beams of spring, I'm free and re-joic-ing — I walk with the King.
you He would bring: Come in-to the sun-light and walk with the King.

I walk with the King, hal-le-lu-jah! I walk with the King, praise His name!

No lon-ger I roam, my soul fac-es home, I walk and I talk with the King.

God Leads Us Along

G. A. YOUNG

G. A. YOUNG

1. In shad - y, green pas - tures, so rich and so sweet, God leads His dear
2. Some - times on the mount where the sun shines so bright, God leads His dear
3. Tho' sor - rows be - fall us and Sa - tan op - pose, God leads His dear
4. A - way from the mire, and a - way from the clay, God leads His dear

chil - dren a - long. Where the wa - ter's cool flow bathes the wea - ry one's feet,
chil - dren a - long. Some - times in the val - ley, in dark - est of night,
chil - dren a - long. Through grace we can con - quer, de - feat all our foes;
chil - dren a - long. A - way up in glo - ry, e - ter - ni - ty's day,

God leads His dear chil - dren a - long. Some thro' the wa - ters, some thro' the flood,

Some thro' the fire, but all thro' the blood; Some thro' great sor - row, but

God gives a song In the night sea - son and all the day long.

89 Wonderful Grace of Jesus

HALDOR LILLENAS   HALDOR LILLENAS

1. Won - der - ful grace of Je - sus, Great - er than all my sin;
2. Won - der - ful grace of Je - sus, Reach - ing to all the lost,
3. Won - der - ful grace of Je - sus, Reach - ing the most de - filed,

How shall my tongue de - scribe it, Where shall its praise be - gin?
By it I have been par - doned, Saved to the ut - ter - most;
By its trans - form - ing pow - er Mak - ing him God's dear child.

Tak - ing a - way my bur - den, Set - ting my spir - it free,
Chains have been torn a - sun - der, Giv - ing me lib - er - ty,
Pur - chas - ing peace and heav - en For all e - ter - ni - ty—

For the won - der - ful grace of Je - sus reach - es me.
For the won - der - ful grace of Je - sus reach - es me.
And the won - der - ful grace of Je - sus reach - es me.

the match - less grace of Je - sus,
Won - der - ful the match - less grace of Je - sus, Deep - er than the

90 Hallelujah for the Cross

HORATIUS BONAR   JAMES McGRANAHAN

1. The cross, it stand-eth fast! Hal-le-lu-jah, hal-le-lu-jah!
2. It is the old cross still! Hal-le-lu-jah, hal-le-lu-jah!
3. 'Twas here the debt was paid! Hal-le-lu-jah, hal-le-lu-jah!

De-fy-ing ev-'ry blast! Hal-le-lu-jah, hal-le-lu-jah!
Its tri-umph let us tell! Hal-le-lu-jah, hal-le-lu-jah!
Our sins on Je-sus laid! Hal-le-lu-jah, hal-le-lu-jah!

The winds of hell have blown, The world its hate hath shown,
The grace of God here shone Thro' Christ, the bless-ed Son,
So round the cross we sing Of Christ, our of-fer-ing,

Yet it is not o-ver-thrown! Hal-le-lu-jah for the cross.
Who did for sin a-tone! Hal-le-lu-jah for the cross.
Of Christ, our liv-ing King! Hal-le-lu-jah for the cross.

The King Is Coming

91

GLORIA GAITHER
WILLIAM J. GAITHER
CHARLES MILLHUFF

WILLIAM J. GAITHER

92

I Won't Have to Cross Jordan Alone

THOMAS RAMSEY

CHARLES E. DURHAM

1. When I come to the riv-er at end-ing of day, When the last winds of
2. Of-ten-times I'm for-sak-en, and wea-ry and sad, When it seems that my
3. Tho' the bil-lows of sor-row and trou-ble may sweep, Christ the Sav-ior will

sor - row have blown;   There'll be some-bod - y wait-ing to show me the way,
friends have all gone;   There is one thought that cheers me and makes my heart glad,
care   for His own;   Till the end   of the jour-ney, my soul He will keep,
winds   of sor-row have blown;

I won't have to cross Jor-dan a - lone.
I won't have   to cross Jor-dan a -
I won't have   to   cross

lone.   Je - sus died for my sins to a - tone;   When the
Jor - dan a - lone.

dark-ness I see, He'll be wait-ing for me,   I won't have to cross Jor-dan a - lone.

Breathe on Me

EDWIN HATCH
Adapt. by B. B. McKinney

B. B. McKINNEY

1. Ho - ly Spir - it, breathe on me, Un - til my heart is clean;
2. Ho - ly Spir - it, breathe on me, My stub - born will sub - due;
3. Ho - ly Spir - it, breathe on me, Fill me with pow'r di - vine;
4. Ho - ly Spir - it, breathe on me, Till I am all Thine own,

Let sun - shine fill its in - most part, With not a cloud be - tween.
Teach me in words of liv - ing flame What Christ would have me do.
Kin - dle a flame of love and zeal With - in this heart of mine.
Un - til my will is lost in Thine, To live for Thee a - lone.

Breathe on me, breathe on me, Ho - ly Spir - it, breathe on me;

Take Thou my heart, cleanse ev - 'ry part, Ho - ly Spir - it, breathe on me.

94 When We See Christ

ESTHER KERR RUSTHOI

ESTHER KERR RUSTHOI

1. Oft - times the day seems long, our tri - als hard to bear, We're tempt - ed
2. Some - times the sky looks dark with not a ray of light, We're tossed and
3. Life's day will soon be o'er, all storms for - ev - er past, We'll cross the

to com - plain, to mur - mur and de - spair; But Christ will soon ap - pear
driv - en on, no hu - man help in sight; But there is one in heav'n
great di - vide to glo - ry, safe at last; We'll share the joys of heav'n—

to catch His Bride a - way, All tears for - ev - er o - ver in
who knows our deep - est care, Let Je - sus solve your prob - lem — just
a harp, a home, a crown, The tempt - er will be ban - ished, we'll

God's e - ter - nal day.
go to Him in prayer. It will be worth it all when we see Je - sus,
lay our bur - den down.

Life's trials will seem so small when we see Christ; One glimpse of His dear face

all sor-row will e-rase, So brave-ly run the race till we see Christ.

AMAZING GRACE! HOW SWEET THE SOUND

A mazing grace—how sweet the sound—That saved a wretch like me!

John Newton wrote those words. He also wrote that he was "once an infidel libertine." These words are inscribed on a church wall where he was buried. In his early life, he had dealt in the British slave trade, making runs to Africa for slaves and carrying them to ports in the Americas. Through the rich mercy of our Lord and Savior Jesus Christ, however, he was "preserved, restored, pardoned, and appointed to preach the faith he had long labored to destroy." In Newton's later years, William Wilberforce, a young member of Parliament and a born-again Christian, came often to Newton for advice and support. Wilberforce was trying to abolish the slave trade on British ships, and he knew Newton's heart from his sermons against slavery. Newton knew firsthand of the horrors and often shared his experience. In that day (late 1700s) slavery was an issue that most politicians dared not approach, but true Christian love demanded a change.

Newton even gave testimony before Prime Minister William Pitt. It took years for the right to prevail, but in 1807 Wilberforce's bill against slavery was passed by Parliament. It was the final year of Newton's life. His last words were "I am a great sinner…and Christ is a great Savior."

96 Brighten the Corner Where You Are

INA DULANY OGDON

CHARLES H. GABRIEL

1. Do not wait un-til some deed of great-ness you may do, Do not
2. Just a-bove are cloud-ed skies that you may help to clear, Let not
3. Here for all your tal-ent you may sure-ly find a need, Here re-

wait to shed your light a-far, To the man-y du-ties ev-er near you
nar-row self your way de-bar, Tho' in-to one heart a-lone may fall your
flect the Bright and Morn-ing Star, E-ven from your hum-ble hand the bread of

now be true, Bright-en the cor-ner where you are.
song of cheer, Bright-en the cor-ner where you are. Bright-en the cor-ner
life may feed, Bright-en the cor-ner where you are.

where you are! Bright-en the cor-ner where you are! Some-one far from

Shine for Je-sus where you are!

har-bor you may glide a-cross the bar, Bright-en the cor-ner where you are.

I Know That My Redeemeth Liveth

JESSIE BROWN POUNDS   JAMES H. FILLMORE

1. I know that my Re-deem-er liv - eth, And on the earth a - gain shall
2. I know His prom-ise nev - er fail - eth, The word He speaks, it can - not
3. I know my man-sion He pre-par - eth, That where He is there I may

stand; I know e - ter - nal life He giv - eth, That grace and
die; Tho' cru - el death my flesh as - sail - eth, Yet I shall
be; O won - drous tho't, for me he car - eth, And He at

pow'r are in His hand.
see Him by and by.   I know, I know   that Je - sus liv - eth,
last will come for me.   I know, I know

And on the earth   a - gain shall stand; I know, I know
     And on the earth   I know, I know

that life He giv - eth, That grace and pow'r   are in His hand.
     That grace and pow'r

98 Just a Little Talk with Jesus

CLEAVANT DERRICKS   CLEAVANT DERRICKS

1. I once was lost in sin but Je-sus took me in, And then a lit-tle
2. Some-times my path seems drear, with-out a ray of cheer, And then a cloud of
3. I may have doubts and fears, my eyes be filled with tears, But Je-sus is a

light from heav-en filled my soul; It bathed my heart in love and wrote my
doubt may hide the light of day; The mists of sin may rise and hide the
Friend who watch-es day and night; I go to Him in prayer, He knows my

name a-bove, And just a lit-tle talk with Je-sus made me whole.
star-ry skies, But just a lit-tle talk with Je-sus clears the way.
ev-'ry care, And just a lit-tle talk with Je-sus makes it right.

have a lit-tle talk with Je-sus, tell Him all a-bout our
Now let us   Let us

trou-bles, hear our faint-est cry, an-swer by and by:
He will   and He will

feel a lit-tle prayer-ful yearn-ing,   heart un-to heav-en is

Now when you   as your

turn-ing,   find a lit-tle talk with Je - sus makes it   right.

You will   it makes it right.

BECAUSE HE LIVES

*B*ill and Gloria Gaither wrote words and music in 1971, shortly after the birth of their son, Benjy. The condition of the world politically, economically, and spiritually gave them great concern. Yet, they both felt the assurance and affirmation that we all can face the unknown future with confidence because Jesus Christ, our Savior lives. At Bill Gaither's request, the tune was named RESURRECTION. (William J. Reynolds, reprinted from HANDBOOK TO *THE BAPTIST HYMNAL*)

100 He Lives

ALFRED H. ACKLEY

ALFRED H. ACKLEY

1. I serve a ris-en Sav-ior, He's in the world to-day;
2. In all the world a-round me I see His lov-ing care,
3. Re-joice, re-joice, O Chris-tian, lift up your voice and sing

I know that He is liv-ing, what-ev-er men may say;
And tho' my heart grows wea-ry I nev-er will de-spair;
E-ter-nal hal-le-lu-jahs to Je-sus Christ the King!

I see His hand of mer-cy, I hear His voice of cheer,
I know that He is lead-ing thro' all the storm-y blast,
The hope of all who seek Him, the help of all who find,

And just the time I need Him, He's al-ways near.
The day of His ap-pear-ing will come at last.
None oth-er is so lov-ing, so good and kind.

He lives, He lives, Christ Je-sus lives to-day! He walks with me and
He lives, He lives,

talks with me a - long life's nar - row way. He lives, He lives, sal -
He lives, He lives,

va - tion to im - part! You ask me how I know He lives: He lives with - in my heart.

Whisper a Prayer

Arr. by John W. Peterson

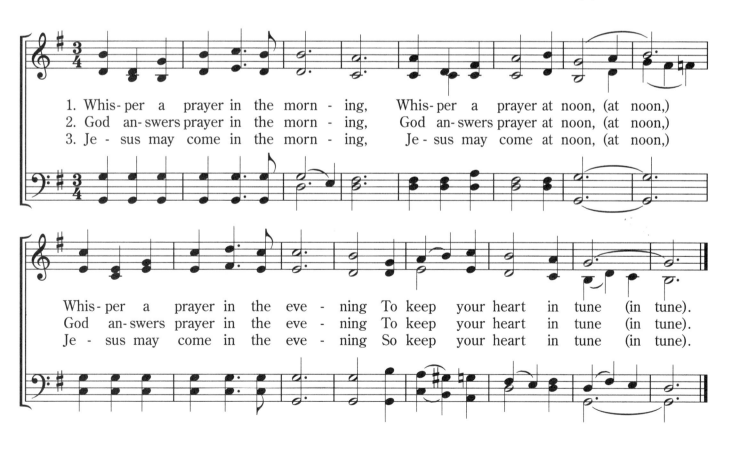

1. Whis - per a prayer in the morn - ing, Whis - per a prayer at noon, (at noon,)
2. God an - swers prayer in the morn - ing, God an - swers prayer at noon, (at noon,)
3. Je - sus may come in the morn - ing, Je - sus may come at noon, (at noon,)

Whis - per a prayer in the eve - ning To keep your heart in tune (in tune).
God an - swers prayer in the eve - ning To keep your heart in tune (in tune).
Je - sus may come in the eve - ning So keep your heart in tune (in tune).

102 He Touched Me

WILLIAM J. GAITHER WILLIAM J. GAITHER

No One Ever Cared for Me Like Jesus　103

CHARLES F. WEIGLE　　　　　　　　　　　　　　　　　　　　CHARLES F. WEIGLE

1. I would love to tell you what I think of Je-sus Since I found in Him a
2. All my life was full of sin when Je-sus found me, All my heart was full of
3. Ev-'ry day He comes to me with new as-sur-ance, More and more I un-der-

friend so strong and true; I would tell you how He changed my life com-plete-ly,
mis-er-y and woe; Je-sus plac'd His strong and lov-ing arms a-round me,
stand His words of love; But I'll nev-er know just why He came to save me,

He did some-thing that no oth-er friend could do.
And He led me in the way I ought to go. No one ev-er cared for
Till some-day I see His bless-ed face a-bove.

me like Je-sus, There's no oth-er friend so kind as He; No one

else could take the sin and dark-ness from me, O how much He cared for me.

104 Who Is on the Lord's Side?

FRANCES RIDLEY HAVERGAL

C. LUISE REICHARDT
Arranged by John Goss

1. Who is on the Lord's side? Who will serve the King? Who will be His help-ers,
2. Je - sus, Thou hast bought us, Not with gold or gem, But with Thine own life- blood,
3. Not for weight of glo - ry, Not for crown and palm, En - ter we His ser - vice,
4. Fierce may be the con - flict, Strong may be the foe, But the King's own ar - my

Oth - er lives to bring? Who will leave the world's side? Who will face the foe?
For Thy di - a - dem. With Thy bless-ing fill - ing Each who comes to Thee,
Raise the con-q'ror's psalm; But for love that claim - eth Lives for whom He died,
None can o - ver - throw. Round His stan-dard rang - ing, Vic - t'ry is se - cure;

Who is on the Lord's side? Who for Him will go? By Thy call of mer - cy,
Thou hast made us will - ing, Thou hast made us free. By Thy grand re - demp-tion,
He whom Je - sus nam - eth Must be on His side. By Thy love con - strain-ing,
For His truth un - chang - ing Makes the tri - umph sure. Joy - ful - ly en - list-ing,

By Thy grace di - vine, We are on the Lord's side, Sav - ior, we are Thine!
By Thy grace di - vine, We are on the Lord's side, Sav - ior, we are Thine!
By Thy grace di - vine, We are on the Lord's side, Sav - ior, we are Thine!
By Thy grace di - vine, We are on the Lord's side, Sav - ior, we are Thine!

Sweet By and By

SANFORD F. BENNETT

JOSEPH P. WEBSTER

106 To God Be the Glory

FANNY J. CROSBY

WILLIAM H. DOANE

1. To God be the glory, great things He hath done; So loved He the
2. O perfect redemption, the purchase of blood, To ev'ry be-
3. Great things He hath taught us, great things He hath done, And great our re-

world that He gave us His Son, Who yielded His life an a-
liever the promise of God; The vilest offender who
joicing thro' Jesus the Son; But purer, and higher, and

tonement for sin, And opened the lifegate that all may go in.
truly believes, That moment from Jesus a pardon receives.
greater will be Our wonder, our vic'try, when Jesus we see.

Praise the Lord, praise the Lord, Let the earth hear His voice! Praise the Lord,

praise the Lord, Let the people rejoice! O come to the Father, thro'

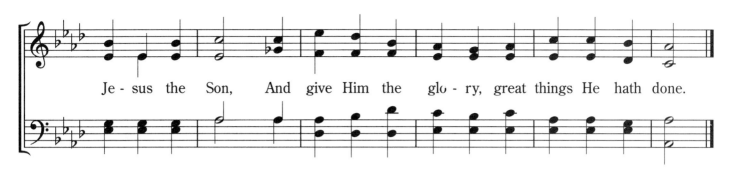

Every Day with Jesus

107

ROBERT C. LOVELESS

WENDELL P. LOVELESS

108 Teach Me to Pray

ALBERT S. REITZ   ALBERT S. REITZ

1. Teach me to pray, Lord, teach me to pray; This is my heart-cry
2. Pow-er in pray'r, Lord, pow-er in pray'r! Here mid earth's sin and
3. My weak-ened will, Lord, Thou canst re-new; My sin-ful na-ture
4. Teach me to pray, Lord, teach me to pray; Thou are my pat-tern

day un-to day; I long to know Thy will and Thy way;
sor-row and care, Men lost and dy-ing, souls in de-spair;
Thou canst sub-due; Fill me just now with pow-er a-new;
day un-to day; Thou art my sure-ty, now and for aye;

Teach me to pray, Lord, teach me to pray.
O give me pow-er, pow-er in pray'r!
Pow-er to pray and pow-er to do!
Teach me to pray, Lord, teach me to pray.   Liv-ing in Thee, Lord,

and Thou in me, Con-stant a-bid-ing, this is my plea; Grant me Thy

pow - er, bound-less and free,   Pow- er with men   and   pow- er with   Thee.

GOD'S PROMISE TO YOU IS ... *REST*

*C*OME unto me, all ye that labour and are heavy laden,
and I will give you rest. Take my yoke upon you, and learn of me;
for I am meek and lowly in heart: and ye shall find rest unto your souls.
For my yoke is easy, and my burden is light.
Matthew 11:28-30 KJV

GOD'S PROMISE TO YOU IS ... *PEACE*

*P*EACE I leave with you, my peace I give unto you:
not as the world giveth, give I unto you.
Let not your heart be troubled, neither let it be afraid.
I will both lay me down in peace, and sleep:
for thou, LORD, only makest me dwell in safety.
John 14:27; Psalm 4:8 KJV

110 Sunrise

W. C. POOLE

B. D. ACKLEY

1. When I shall come to the end of my way, When I shall rest at the
2. When in His beau-ty I see the great King, Join with the ran-somed His
3. When life is o-ver and day-light is passed, In heav-en's har-bor my

close of life's day, When "Wel-come home" I shall hear Je-sus say, O
prais-es to sing, When I shall join them my trib-utes to bring, O
an-chor is cast, When I see Je-sus my Sav-ior at last, O

me.

that will be sun-rise for
that will be sun-rise for sun-rise for me. Sun-rise to-mor-row,
that will be sun-rise for

me.

sun-rise to-mor-row, Sun-rise in glo-ry is wait-ing for me; Sun-rise to-

mor-row, sun-rise to-mor-row, Sun-rise with Je-sus for e-ter-ni-ty.

Sweet Hour of Prayer

WILLIAM WALFORD   WILLIAM B. BRADBURY

1. Sweet hour of prayer, sweet hour of prayer, That calls me from a world of care And
2. Sweet hour of prayer, sweet hour of prayer, Thy wings shall my pe - ti - tion bear To
3. Sweet hour of prayer, sweet hour of prayer, May I Thy con - so - la - tion share, Till,

bids me at my Fa - ther's throne Make all my wants and wish - es known! In
Him whose truth and faith - ful - ness En - gage the wait - ing soul to bless: And
from Mount Pis - gah's loft - y height, I view my home and take my flight: This

sea - sons of dis - tress and grief, My soul has of - ten found re - lief, And
since He bids me seek His face, Be - lieve His word and trust His grace, I'll
robe of flesh I'll drop and rise To seize the ev - er - last - ing prize; And

oft es - caped the tempt - er's snare By Thy re - turn, sweet hour of prayer.
cast on Him my ev - 'ry care, And wait for Thee, sweet hour of prayer.
shout, while pass - ing thro' the air, "Fare - well, fare - well, sweet hour of prayer!"

112

Peace! Be Still!

MARY A. BAKER

HORATIO R. PALMER

1. Mas-ter, the tem-pest is rag-ing! The bil-lows are toss-ing high!
2. Mas-ter, with an-guish of spir-it I bow in my grief to-day;
3. Mas-ter, the ter-ror is o-ver, The el-e-ments sweet-ly rest;

The sky is o'er-shad-owed with black-ness, No shel-ter or help is nigh;
The depths of my sad heart are trou-bled; O wak-en and save, I pray!
Earth's sun in the calm lake is mir-rored, And heav-en's with-in my breast.

"Car-est Thou not that we per-ish?" How canst Thou lie a-sleep,
Tor-rents of sin and of an-guish Sweep o'er my sink-ing soul!
Lin-ger, O bless-ed Re-deem-er, Leave me a-lone no more;

When each mo-ment so mad-ly is threat-'ning A grave in the an-gry deep?
And I per-ish! I per-ish, dear Mas-ter; O has-ten, and take con-trol!
And with joy I shall make the blest har-bor, And rest on the bliss-ful shore.

113 Count Your Blessings

JOHNSON OATMAN, Jr.

EDWIN O. EXCELL

1. When up-on life's bil-lows you are tem-pest tossed, When you are dis-
2. Are you ev-er bur-dened with a load of care? Does the cross seem
3. When you look at oth-ers with their lands and gold, Think that Christ has
4. So, a-mid the con-flict, wheth-er great or small, Do not be dis-

cour-aged, think-ing all is lost, Count your man-y bless-ings, name them
heav-y you are called to bear? Count your man-y bless-ings, ev-'ry
prom-ised you His wealth un-told; Count your man-y bless-ings, mon-ey
cour-aged, God is o-ver all; Count your man-y bless-ings, an-gels

one by one, And it will sur-prise you what the Lord hath done.
doubt will fly, And you will be sing-ing as the days go by.
can-not buy Your re-ward in heav-en, nor your home on high.
will at-tend, Help and com-fort give you to your jour-ney's end.

Count your bless-ings, name them one by one; Count your
Count your man-y bless-ings, name them one by one; Count your man-y

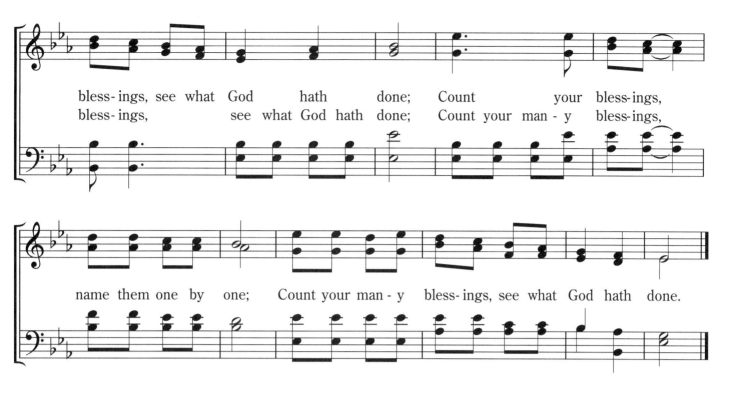

bless-ings, see what God hath done; Count your bless-ings,
bless-ings, see what God hath done; Count your man - y bless-ings,

name them one by one; Count your man - y bless-ings, see what God hath done.

114

GOD'S PROMISE TO YOU IS ... *SALVATION*

FOR God so loved the world,
that he gave his only begotten Son,
that whosoever believeth in him
should not perish, but have everlasting life.
John 3:16 KJV

GOD'S PROMISE TO YOU IS ... *FORGIVENESS*

BLESS the LORD, O my soul,
and forget not all his benefits:
Who forgiveth all thine iniquities;
who healeth all thy diseases;
Who redeemeth thy life from destruction;
who crowneth thee with lovingkindness and tender mercies.
Psalm 103:2-4 KJV

115 He Ransomed Me

JULIA H. JOHNSTON

J. W. HENDERSON

1. There's a sweet and bless-ed sto-ry Of the Christ who came from glo-ry,
2. From the depth of sin and sad-ness To the heights of joy and glad-ness
3. From the throne of heav'n-ly glo-ry O the sweet and bless-ed sto-ry!
4. By and by with joy in-creas-ing, And with grat-i-tude un-ceas-ing,

Just to res-cue me from sin and mis-er-y; He in lov-ing kind-ness sought me,
Je-sus lift-ed me, in mer-cy full and free; With His pre-cious blood He bought me,
Je-sus came to lift the lost in sin and woe In-to lib-er-ty all-glo-rious,
Lift-ed up with Christ for-ev-er-more to be; I will join the hosts there sing-ing,

And from sin and shame hath bro't me, Hal-le-lu-jah! Je-sus ran-somed me.
When I knew Him not, He sought me, And in love di-vine He ran-somed me.
Tro-phies of His grace vic-to-rious, Ev-er-more re-joic-ing here be-low.
In the an-them ev-er ring-ing, To the King of Love who ran-somed me.

Hal-le-lu-jah, what a Sav-ior! Who can take a poor lost sin-ner, Lift him

from the mir-y clay and set him free; (Hal-le-lu-jah!) I will ev-er tell the sto-ry,

Shout - ing glo - ry, glo - ry, glo - ry, Hal - le - lu - jah! Je - sus ran - somed me.

Heavenly Sunshine

116

H. J. ZELLEY

GEORGE HARRISON COOK
Arranged by Charles E. Fuller

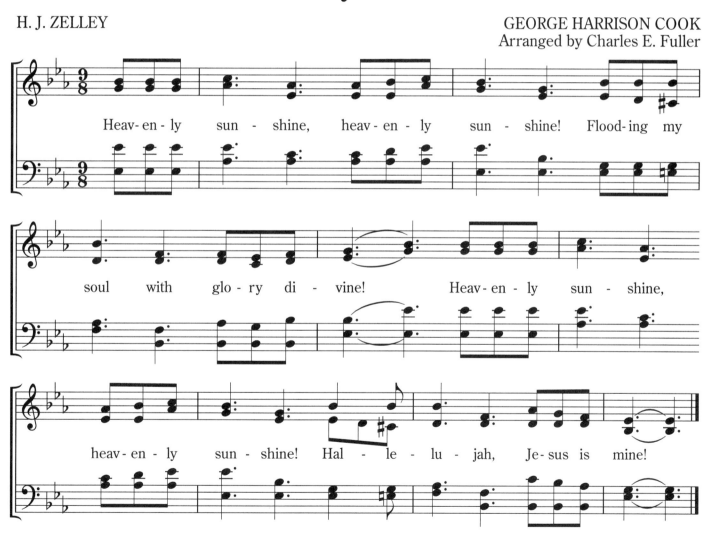

Heav - en - ly sun - shine, heav - en - ly sun - shine! Flood - ing my

soul with glo - ry di - vine! Heav - en - ly sun - shine,

heav - en - ly sun - shine! Hal - le - lu - jah, Je - sus is mine!

117 One Day

J. WILBUR CHAPMAN

CHARLES H. MARSH

1. One day when heav - en was filled with His prais - es, One day when
2. One day they led Him up Cal - va - ry's moun - tain, One day they
3. One day they left Him a - lone in the gar - den, One day He
4. One day the grave could con - ceal Him no lon - ger, One day the
5. One day the trum - pet will sound for His com - ing, One day the

sin was as black as could be, Je - sus came forth to be
nailed Him to die on the tree; Suf - fer - ing an - guish, de -
rest - ed, from suf - fer - ing free; An - gels came down o'er His
stone rolled a - way from the door; Then He a - rose, o - ver
skies with His glo - ries will shine; Won - der - ful day, my be -

born of a vir - gin, Dwelt a - mong men, my ex - am - ple is He!
spised and re - ject - ed: Bear - ing our sins, my Re - deem - er is He!
tomb to keep vig - il; Hope of the hope - less, my Sav - ior is He!
death He had con - quered; Now is as - cend - ed, my Lord ev - er - more!
lov - ed One bring - ing; Glo - ri - ous Sav - ior, this Je - sus is mine!

Liv - ing, He loved me; dy - ing, He saved me; Bur - ied, He

car - ried my sins far a - way; Ris - ing, He jus - ti - fied

free - ly for - ev - er: One day He's com - ing — O glo - ri - ous day!

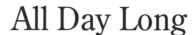

All Day Long

African Folk Hymn

Traditional
Arr. by Marie Gray

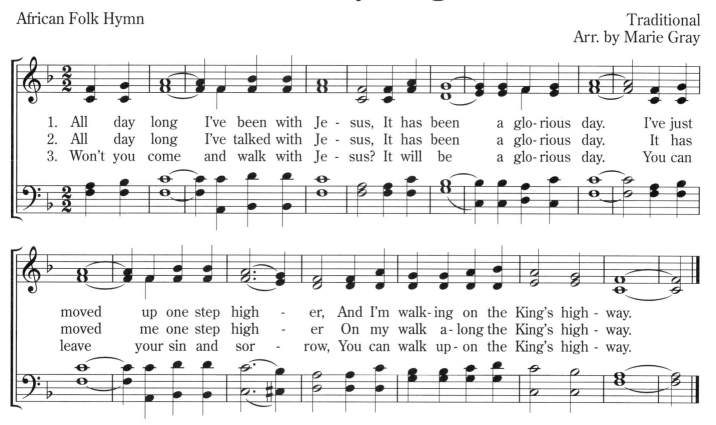

1. All day long I've been with Je - sus, It has been a glo - rious day. I've just
2. All day long I've talked with Je - sus, It has been a glo - rious day. It has
3. Won't you come and walk with Je - sus? It will be a glo - rious day. You can

moved up one step high - er, And I'm walk - ing on the King's high - way.
moved me one step high - er On my walk a - long the King's high - way.
leave your sin and sor - row, You can walk up - on the King's high - way.

119 Nearer, My God, to Thee

SARAH F. ADAMS

LOWELL MASON

1. Near - er, my God, to Thee, Near - er to Thee!
2. There let the way ap - pear, Steps un - to heav'n;
3. Then with my wak - ing tho'ts Bright with Thy praise,

E'en tho' it be a cross That rais - eth me;
All that Thou send - est me, In mer - cy giv'n;
Out of my ston - y griefs Beth - el I'll raise;

Still all my song shall be, Near - er, my God, to Thee!
An - gels to beck - on me Near - er, my God, to Thee!
So by my woes to be Near - er, my God, to Thee!

Near - er, my God, to Thee, Near - er to Thee!
Near - er, my God, to Thee, Near - er to Thee!
Near - er, my God, to Thee, Near - er to Thee!

Savior, More than Life to Me

FANNY J. CROSBY

WILLIAM H. DOANE

1. Sav - ior, more than life to me, I am cling- ing, cling- ing close to Thee;
2. Thro' this chang - ing world be - low, Lead me gen - tly, gen - tly as I go;
3. Let me love Thee more and more, Till this fleet- ing, fleet- ing life is o'er;

Let Thy pre - cious blood ap - plied, Keep me ev - er, ev - er near Thy side.
Trust- ing Thee, I can - not stray, I can nev - er, nev - er lose my way.
Till my soul is lost in love, In a bright- er, bright- er world a - bove.

Ev - 'ry day, ev - 'ry hour, Let me feel Thy cleans- ing pow'r;
Ev - 'ry day and hour, ev - 'ry day and hour,

May Thy ten - der love to me Bind me clos- er, clos- er, Lord, to Thee.

121 There'll Be Peace in the Valley

THOMAS A. DORSEY

THOMAS A. DORSEY
Arranged by Joseph Linn

1. Well, I'm tired and so wea - ry, but I must toil on
2. There the flow'rs will be bloom - ing, and the grass will be green,
3. Well, the bear will be gen - tle, and the wolf will be tame,

Till the Lord comes and calls me a - way, oh, yes.
And the skies will be clear and se - rene, oh, yes.
And the lion shall lay down by the lamb, oh, yes.

Well, the morn - ing is bright and the Lamb is the Light,
Well, the sun ev - er beams in the val - ley of dreams,
Well, the beast from the wild shall be led by a child,

And the night, night is as fair as the day, oh, yes.
And no clouds there will ev - er be seen, oh, yes.
And I'll be changed, changed from this crea - ture that I am, oh, yes.

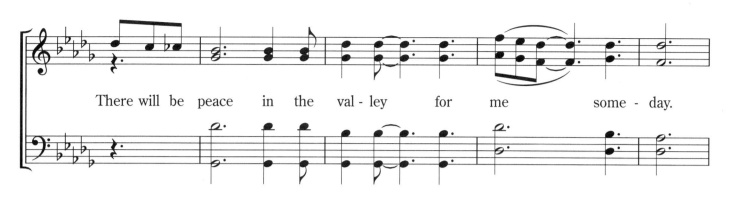

There will be peace in the val - ley for me some - day.

There will be peace in the val - ley for me, O Lord, I pray.

There'll be no sad-ness, no sor - row, no trou-ble I'll see.

no sor - row, O my Lord-y, no trou-ble, trou-ble I'll see.

There will be peace in the val - ley for me.

me, for me.

122 God Will Take Care of You

CIVILLA D. MARTIN

W. STILLMAN MARTIN

1. Be not dis-mayed what-e'er be-tide, God will take care of you;
2. Thro' days of toil when heart doth fail, God will take care of you;
3. No mat-ter what may be the test, God will take care of you;

Be-neath His wings of love a-bide, God will take care of you.
When dan-gers fierce your path as-sail, God will take care of you.
Lean, wea-ry one, up-on His breast, God will take care of you.

God will take care of you, Through ev-'ry day, o'er all the way;

He will take care of you, God will take care of you.

Guide Me, O Thou Great Jehovah

WILLIAM WILLIAMS   THOMAS HASTINGS

1. Guide me, O Thou great Je - ho - vah, Pil - grim thro' this bar - ren land;
2. O - pen now the crys - tal foun - tain, Whence the heal - ing wa - ters flow;
3. When I tread the verge of Jor - dan, Bid my anx - ious fears sub - side;

I am weak, but Thou art might - y, Hold me with Thy pow'r - ful hand;
Let the fire and cloud - y pil - lar Lead me all my jour - ney thro';
Bear me through the swell - ing cur - rent, Land me safe on Ca - naan's side;

Bread of heav - en, Feed me till I want no more;
Strong De - liv - er - er, Be Thou still my strength and shield;
Songs of prais - es I will ev - er give to Thee;

Bread of heav - en, Feed me till I want no more.
Strong De - liv - er - er, Be Thou still my strength and shield.
Songs of prais - es I will ev - er give to Thee.

124 Fill My Cup

RICHARD BLANCHARD

RICHARD BLANCHARD

1. Like the wo-man at the well I was seek-ing For things that
2. There are mil-lions in this world who are crav-ing The plea-sure
3. So, my broth-er, if the things this world gave you Leave hun-gers

could not sat-is-fy; And then I heard my Sav-ior speak-ing "Draw
earth-ly things af-ford; But none can match the won-drous trea-sure
that won't pass a-way, My bless-ed Lord will come and save you,

from My well that nev-er shall run dry."
That I find in Je-sus Christ my Lord. Fill my cup, Lord, I lift it
If you kneel to Him and hum-bly pray:

up, Lord! Come and quench this thirst-ing of my soul. Bread of heav-en,

feed me till I want no more, Fill my cup, fill it up and make me whole!

VIRGIL P. BROCK

BLANCHE KERR BROCK

126 Whispering Hope

ALICE HAWTHORNE   ALICE HAWTHORNE

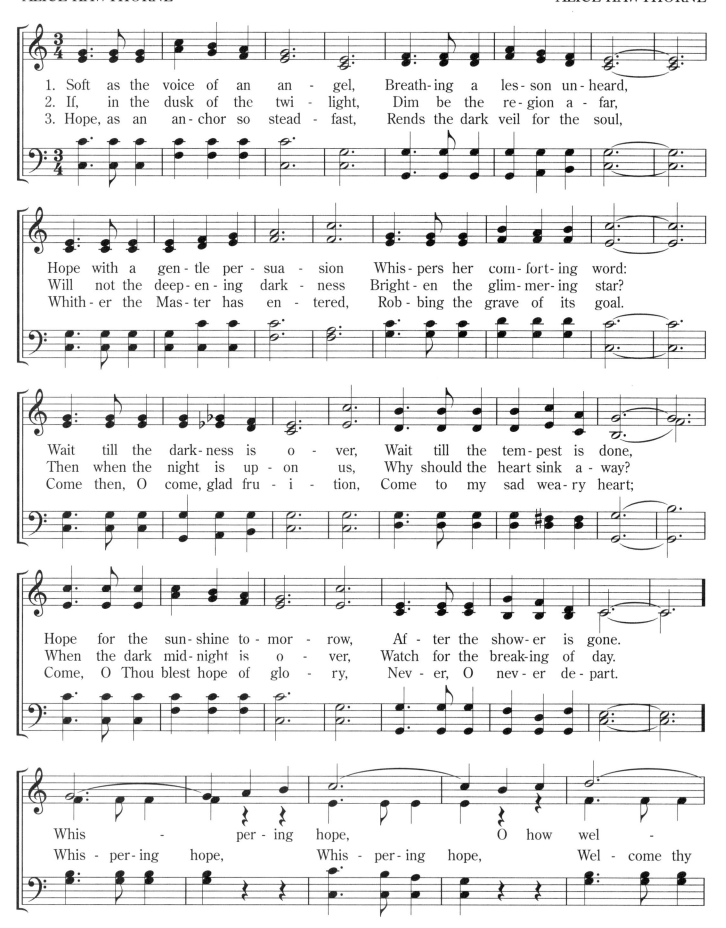

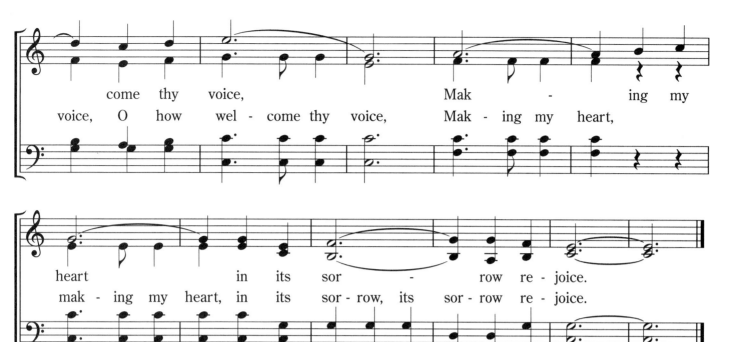

come thy voice,   Mak - ing my
voice, O how wel - come thy voice,   Mak - ing my heart,

heart   in its sor - row re - joice.
mak - ing my heart, in its sor - row, its sor - row re - joice.

GOD'S PROMISE TO YOU IS ... STRENGTH

THE LORD is my light and my salvation; whom shall I fear?
the LORD is the strength of my life; of whom shall I be afraid?
I will strengthen thee; yea, I will help thee;
yea, I will uphold thee with the right hand of my righteousness.
Psalm 27:1; Isaiah 41:10 KJV

GOD'S PROMISE TO YOU IS ... SECURITY

MY sheep hear my voice, and I know them, and they follow me:
And I give unto them eternal life; and they shall never perish.
My Father, which gave them me,
is greater than all; and no man
is able to pluck them out of my Father's hand.
John 10:27-29 KJV

128 Follow, I Will Follow Thee

HOWARD L. BROWN
and MARGARET W. BROWN

HOWARD L. BROWN
Arr. by HERBERT G. TOVEY

Loyalty to Christ

129

Dr. E. T. CASSEL

FLORA H. CASSEL

1. From o-ver hill and plain There comes the sig-nal strain, 'Tis loy-al-ty, loy-al-ty,
2. O hear, ye brave, the sound That moves the earth a-round, 'Tis loy-al-ty, loy-al-ty,
3. Come, join our loy-al throng, We'll rout the gi-ant wrong, 'Tis loy-al-ty, loy-al-ty,
4. The strength of youth we lay At Je-sus' feet to-day, 'Tis loy-al-ty, loy-al-ty,

loy-al-ty to Christ; Its mu-sic rolls a-long, The hills take up the song,
loy-al-ty to Christ; A-rise to dare and do, Ring out the watch-word true,
loy-al-ty to Christ; Where Sa-tan's ban-ners float We'll send the bu-gle note,
loy-al-ty to Christ; His Gos-pel we'll pro-claim Thro'-out the world's do-main,

Of loy-al-ty, loy-al-ty, Yes, loy-al-ty to Christ. "On to vic-to-ry! On to

vic-to-ry!" Cries our great Com-man-der, "On!" We'll move at His com-mand,
great Com-man-der, "On!"

We'll soon pos-sess the land, Thro' loy-al-ty, loy-al-ty, Yes, loy-al-ty to Christ.

130 At Calvary

WILLIAM R. NEWELL

DANIEL B. TOWNER

1. Years I spent in van - i - ty and pride, Car - ing not my Lord was cru - ci - fied, Know - ing not it was for me He died On Cal - va - ry.
2. By God's Word at last my sin I learned; Then I trem - bled at the law I'd spurned, Till my guilt - y soul im - plor - ing turned To Cal - va - ry.
3. Now I've giv'n to Je - sus ev - 'ry - thing, Now I glad - ly own Him as my King, Now my rap - tured soul can on - ly sing Of Cal - va - ry.
4. Oh, the love that drew sal - va - tion's plan! Oh, the grace that bro't it down to man! Oh, the might - y gulf that God did span At Cal - va - ry.

Mer - cy there was great, and grace was free; Par - don there was mul - ti - plied to me; There my bur - dened soul found lib - er - ty At Cal - va - ry.

There's Something About That Name 131

WILLIAM J. GAITHER
and GLORIA GAITHER

WILLIAM J. GAITHER

Je - sus, Je - sus, Je - sus; There's just some - thing a - bout that

name! Mas - ter, Sav - ior, Je - sus, Like the fra - grance

af - ter the rain; Je - sus, Je - sus, Je - sus, Let all

heav - en and earth pro - claim: Kings and king - doms will

all pass a - way, But there's some - thing a - bout that name!

132 Sweet, Sweet Spirit

DORIS AKERS
Arr. by Kurt Kaiser

DORIS AKERS
Arr. by Kurt Kaiser

* Author's original word is "stay."

bless-ings We lift our hearts in praise; With-out a doubt we'll know that

we have been re-vived When we shall leave this place.

HE LIVES

*I*n 1933, Alfred H. Ackley was witnessing to a young Jew and was asked, "Why should I worship a dead Jew?"

Ackley replied, "He lives! I tell you, He is not dead, but lives here and now! Jesus Christ is more alive today than ever before." After this encounter, Ackley produced the words and music of "He Lives" as well as a sermon on the subject of Jesus' resurrection. (Paul G. Hammond, reprinted from HANDBOOK TO *THE BAPTIST HYMNAL*)

134 Love Lifted Me

JAMES ROWE

HOWARD E. SMITH

1. I was sink-ing deep in sin, far from the peace-ful shore, Ver-y deep-ly stained with-in, sink-ing to rise no more; But the Mas-ter of the sea heard my de-spair-ing cry, From the wa-ters lift-ed me, now safe am I.

2. All my heart to Him I give, ev-er to Him I'll cling, In His bless-ed pres-ence live, ev-er His prais-es sing; Love so might-y and so true mer-its my soul's best songs; Faith-ful lov-ing ser-vice, too, to Him be-longs.

3. Souls in dan-ger, look a-bove, Je-sus com-plete-ly saves; He will lift you by His love out of the an-gry waves; He's the Mas-ter of the sea, bil-lows His will o-bey; He your Sav-ior wants to be, be saved to-day.

Love lift-ed me! Love lift-ed me! When noth-ing e-ven me! e-ven me! else could help, Love lift-ed me. Love lift-ed me.

At the Cross

ISAAC WATTS
RALPH E. HUDSON, Refrain

RALPH E. HUDSON

1. A - las, and did my Sav - ior bleed, And did my Sov - 'reign die?
2. Was it for crimes that I had done He groaned up - on the tree?
3. Well might the sun in dark - ness hide, And shut His glo - ries in,
4. Thus might I hide my blush - ing face While Cal - v'ry's cross ap - pears,
5. But drops of grief can ne'er re - pay The debt of love I owe;

Would He de - vote that sa - cred head For sin - ners such as I?
A - maz - ing pit - y, grace un - known, And love be - yond de - gree!
When Christ the might - y Mak - er died For man, the crea - ture's sin.
Dis - solve my heart in thank - ful - ness, And melt mine eyes to tears.
Here, Lord, I give my - self a - way, 'Tis all that I can do.

At the cross, at the cross where I first saw the light, And the

bur - den of my heart rolled a - way, (rolled a - way,) It was there by faith

I re - ceived my sight, And now I am hap - py all the day!

TOPICAL INDEX

ASSURANCE
A Mighty Fortress Is Our God, 18 (C)
Amazing Grace! How Sweet the
   Sound, 5 (G)
Beulah Land, 1 (F)
Blessed Assurance, Jesus Is
   Mine, 10 (D)
Each Step I Take, 44 (Eb)
God Will Take Care of You, 122 (Bb)
His Eye Is on the Sparrow, 50 (C)
In the Garden, 80 (Ab)
It Is Well with My Soul, 81 (Db)
Love Lifted Me, 134 (Bb)
My God and I, 60 (C)
Precious Memories, 6 (Ab)
Under His Wings, 30 (C)

BENEDICTIONS
God Be with You, 36 (Bb)
Sweet, Sweet Spirit, 132 (G)

BLOOD OF JESUS CHRIST
At the Cross, 135 (Eb)
The Old Rugged Cross, 39 (Bb)
To God Be the Glory, 106 (Ab)
Victory in Jesus, 48 (G)
When I See the Blood, 69 (C)

CHRISTMAS
Away in a Manger, 19 (F)
Joy to the World! The Lord Is
   Come, 20 (D)
O Come, All Ye Faithful, 21 (G)
Silent Night, Holy Night, 22 (Bb)

COMFORT AND GUIDANCE
A Shelter in the Time of Storm, 79 (F)
Because He Lives, 61 (Ab)
Blessed Assurance, Jesus Is Mine, 10 (D)
Count Your Blessings, 113 (Eb)
Does Jesus Care?, 71 (C)
God Leads Us Along, 88 (Db)
God Will Take Care of You, 122 (Bb)
Great Is Thy Faithfulness, 65 (Eb)
Guide Me, O Thou Great
   Jehovah, 123 (C)
He Lives, 100 (Bb)

In the Garden, 80 (Ab)
It Is Well with My Soul, 81 (Db)
Love Lifted Me, 134 (Bb)
Never Alone, 2 (Bb)
No, Not One, 54 (F)
Precious Memories, 6 (Ab)
Stepping in the Light, 13 (C)
Surely Goodness and Mercy, 32 (Eb)
Sweet Hour of Prayer, 111 (C)
Sweet Peace, the Gift of God's
   Love, 57 (Ab)
To God Be the Glory, 106 (Ab)
Trust and Obey, 16 (F)
What a Friend We Have in Jesus, 86 (F)

COMMITMENT AND CONSECRATION
"Are Ye Able," Said the Master, 55 (Ab)
Breathe on Me, 93 (Eb)
Fill My Cup, 124 (Bb)
Follow, I Will Follow Thee, 128 (G)
Follow On, 26 (G)
In Times Like These, 17 (Ab)
Lord, Send a Revival, 49 (chorus) (Ab)
Nearer, My God, to Thee, 119 (G)
Savior, More than Life to Me, 120 (Ab)
The Longer I Serve Him, 76 (Ab)
Work, for the Night Is Coming, 59 (F)

CROSS OF JESUS CHRIST
At Calvary, 130 (C)
At the Cross, 135 (Eb)
Hallelujah for the Cross, 90 (Bb)
How Great Thou Art, 42 (Bb)
One Day, 117 (Db)
The Old Rugged Cross, 39 (Bb)
Victory in Jesus, 48 (G)

ETERNAL LIFE
A New Name in Glory, 14 (Bb)
Amazing Grace! How Sweet the
   Sound, 5 (G)
How Great Thou Art, 42 (Bb)
I Know That My Redeemer
   Liveth, 97 (C)
Nearer, My God, to Thee, 119 (G)
Sweet By and By, 105 (G)

Sweet Hour of Prayer, 111 (C)
When We All Get to Heaven, 70 (C)
When the Roll Is Called Up
   Yonder, 52 (Ab)

EVANGELISM
At Calvary, 130 (C)
At the Cross, 135 (Eb)
Because He Lives, 61 (Ab)
Blessed Assurance, Jesus Is Mine, 10 (D)
Bring Them In, 25 (Ab)
Bringing in the Sheaves, 40 (Bb)
He Lives, 100 (Bb)
I Know That My Redeemer
   Liveth, 97 (C)
It Is Well with My Soul, 81 (Db)
Lord, Send a Revival, 49 (chorus) (Ab)
Love Lifted Me, 134 (Bb)
Surely Goodness and Mercy, 32 (Eb)

FAITH, HOPE, AND TRUST
At the Cross, 135 (Eb)
Be Still, My Soul, 78 (F)
Beulah Land, 1 (F)
Blessed Assurance, Jesus Is Mine, 10 (D)
Each Step I Take, 44 (Eb)
Great Is Thy Faithfulness, 65 (Eb)
Guide Me, O Thou Great
   Jehovah, 123 (C)
Heaven Came Down, 58 (F)
Peace! Be Still!, 112 (C)
Surely Goodness and Mercy, 32 (Eb)
Whispering Hope, 126 (C)
Wonderful Peace, 75 (G)

FRIEND-JESUS CHRIST
Anywhere with Jesus, 83 (D)
Every Day with Jesus, 107 (chorus) (F)
Heaven Came Down, 58 (F)
He's a Wonderful Savior to
   Me, 125 (Db)
Just a Little Talk with Jesus, 98 (Bb)
No, Not One, 54 (F)
No One Ever Cared for Me Like
   Jesus, 103 (Db)
What a Friend We Have in Jesus, 86 (F)

TITLE INDEX